JAMES LIMBURG

JONAH

JAMES LIMBURG

JONAH

A Commentary

Westminster/John Knox Press
Louisville, Kentucky

For Acknowledgments, see page 11.

First edition

Published by Westminster/John Knox Press
Louisville, Kentucky

This book is printed on acid-free paper that meets the American National Standards Institute Z39.48 standard. ∞

PRINTED IN THE UNITED STATES OF AMERICA

9 8 7 6 5 4 3 2 1

Library of Congress Cataloging-in-Publication Data

Limburg, James, 1935–
    Jonah : a commentary / James Limburg. — 1st ed.
        p.   cm.—(The Old Testament library)
    Includes bibliographical references.
    ISBN 0-664-21296-4 (alk. paper)
    1. Bible. O.T. Jonah—Commentaries. I. Bible. O.T. Jonah.
English.   New Revised Standard.   1993.   II. Title   III. Series.
BS1605.3.L565   1993
224'.92077—dc20   93-17160

To My Students

Who Have Made Three Decades of Teaching
a Challenge and a Joy

CONTENTS

PREFACE

"Jonah is everywhere," remarked one of the students after a session of our Jonah seminar at the University of Munich in the spring of 1991. Indeed. We had been talking about representations of the Jonah story in stained-glass windows, sculptures, musicals, dramas, even in the sign hanging outside the Gasthaus zum Walfisch in nearby Regensburg. That evening the student had noticed a poster on the wall of the university building advertising a new Jonah dramatization in a Munich theater.

The book of Jonah has never been the exclusive property of theologians or members of religious communities. The incident involving the prophet and the great fish has captured the imagination of poets and novelists, painters and dramatists, sculptors and songwriters, architects and toy makers, to a degree matched by few stories in or out of the Bible.

The aim of this commentary is to explain the biblical book of Jonah and to indicate its importance for our own time. In carrying out that assignment, I have learned much from theologians who have written on this book. However, I have also learned from other, less traditional interpreters of Jonah.

During a sabbatical year in Germany, my wife and I saw the massive Jonah window in the church at Gouda in the Netherlands, the Jonah windows in the cathedral at Cologne (as well as the Jonah door handle there!), the unforgettable whale pulpit in the church at Duszniki Zdroj in southwestern Poland. In addition to these examples, there is the colorful Jonah fountain near Augsburg, Germany, with a mosaic by Walter Habdank, the playful Jonah in a fountain designed by Carl Milles at the Cranbrook Academy of Art in Michigan, a terrified Jonah in a painting by Albert Pinkham Ryder at the National Museum of American Art in Washington, D.C., a musical setting of a Middle English poem, "Jonah and the Whale," by Dominick Argento of the University of Minnesota, a series of Jonah sketches by Marc Chagall. The list goes on. That student was right. Jonah is everywhere.

I want to thank a number of those who have helped with this project. James Luther Mays invited me to write on Jonah in this series and has remained an encouragement along the way. Luther Northwestern Theological Seminary made possible a sabbatical year in Germany, and Lutheran Brotherhood assisted with a financial grant. Frau Dora Goppelt of Tutzing, Bavaria, not only provided a home for my wife and me but also was a good friend and a built-in German teacher. Professor Jörg Jeremias of the University of Munich shared his office, made available the resources of the theological library, and invited me to teach a seminar on Jonah with him. My wife, Martha, was always willing to take one more train trip to find a new Jonah window or Jonah sculpture, and provided her usual balance of encouragement and editorial critique. Back home in St. Paul, Nancy Richmond, my assistant, checked the biblical references and also made some valuable suggestions.

As I finished this project, I realized that I have now completed three decades of teaching, at a college, a seminary, and a university—as well as in an assortment of churches and synagogues, camps and retreats. The dedication intends to thank all those who have studied the Bible with me, for what I have learned from them, and for the good times we have had together.

                                                              J. L.

Woman Lake, Minnesota
Summer 1992

ACKNOWLEDGMENTS

Grateful acknowledgment is made to the following for permission to reproduce copyrighted material.

Concordia Publishing House, from *Luther's Works* (volume 19), Copyright 1974 Concordia Publishing House. Used by permission from Concordia Publishing House.

Doubleday & Co. from *The Old Testament Pseudepigrapha,* by James H. Charlesworth. Copyright © 1983, 1985 by James H. Charlesworth. Used by permission of Doubleday, a division of Bantam Doubleday Dell Publishing Group, Inc.

Reece Halsey Agency, from Aldous Huxley, "Jonah."

Georg Olms Verlag, Hildesheim, from August Wünsche, *Aus Israels Lehrhallen,* volume II, 1967.

Soncino Press, Ltd., from *The Zohar,* volume IV, first published 1934.

ABBREVIATIONS

AB	Anchor Bible
ABD	*The Anchor Bible Dictionary.* 6 vols. Garden City, N.Y.: Doubleday & Co., 1992
ANET	*Ancient Near Eastern Texts Relating to the Old Testament,* ed. J. B. Pritchard. Princeton: Princeton University Press, 1969[3]
BAGD[2]	W. Bauer, W. F. Arndt, F. W. Gingrich, and F. W. Danker, *Greek-English Lexicon of the New Testament.* Chicago: University of Chicago Press, 1979[2]
BASOR	*Bulletin of the American Schools of Oriental Research*
BDB	F. Brown, S. R. Driver, and C. A. Briggs, *Hebrew and English Lexicon of the Old Testament.* Oxford: Clarendon Press, 1978
BHS	*Biblia Hebraica Stuttgartensia,* ed. K. Elliger and W. Rudolph. Stuttgart, 1984[2]
BIOSCS	*Bulletin of the International Organization for Septuagint and Cognate Studies*
BKAT	Biblischer Kommentar: Altes Testament
BN	*Biblische Notizen*
BZ	*Biblische Zeitschrift*
DJD	Discoveries in the Judaean Desert
GKC	*Gesenius' Hebrew Grammar,* ed. E. Kautzsch; trans. A. E. Cowley. 2nd Eng. ed. (Oxford, 1910)
HAR	*Hebrew Annual Review*
IDB	*Interpreter's Dictionary of the Bible.* 4 vols., ed. G. A. Buttrick. Nashville: Abingdon Press, 1962
IDBSup	*Interpreter's Dictionary of the Bible,* Supplementary Volume, ed. K. Crim. Nashville: Abingdon Press, 1976
JPS	*Tanakh: The Holy Scriptures.* Philadelphia: Jewish Publication Society, 1985
JSOT	*Journal for the Study of the Old Testament*
KB	L. Koehler and W. Baumgartner, *Lexicon in Veteris Testamenti libros*
KB[3]	W. Baumgartner and others, *Hebräisches und Aramäisches Lexikon zum Alten Testament,* Lieferung I. Leiden: E. J. Brill, 1967
MT	Masoretic text

OTP   *The Old Testament Pseudepigrapha,* ed. J. H. Charlesworth.
         2 vols. Garden City, N.Y.: Doubleday & Co., 1983, 1985

PRE   *Pirķê de Rabbi Eliezer,* ed. and trans. G. Friedlander. New
         York: Benjamin Blom, 1971

TDNT   *Theological Dictionary of the New Testament,* ed. G. Kittel and
         G. Friedrich

VT   *Vetus Testamentum*

WMANT   Wissenschaftliche Monographien zum Alten und Neuen
         Testament

ZAW   *Zeitschrift für die alttestamentliche Wissenschaft*

SELECTED BIBLIOGRAPHY

1. Commentaries

Allen, L. C. *The Books of Joel, Obadiah, Jonah, and Micah.* New International Commentary on the Old Testament. Grand Rapids: Wm. B. Eerdmans Publishing Co., 1976.

Calvin, J. *Commentaries on the Minor Prophets.* Translated by John Owen. Grand Rapids: Baker Book House, 1979.

Fretheim, T. *The Message of Jonah: A Theological Commentary.* Minneapolis: Augsburg Publishing House, 1977.

Limburg, J. *Hosea–Micah.* Interpretation: A Bible Commentary for Teaching and Preaching. Atlanta: John Knox Press, 1988.

Luther, M. *Jonah, Habakkuk.* Edited by H. C. Oswald. Luther's Works 19. St. Louis: Concordia Publishing House, 1974.

Rudolph, W. *Joel–Amos–Obadja–Jona.* Kommentar zum Alten Testament 13/2. Gütersloh: Gütersloher Verlagshaus Gerd Mohn, 1971.

Sasson, J. M. *Jonah.* Anchor Bible 24B. Garden City, N.Y.: Doubleday & Co., 1990. Note the complete bibliography, 31–62.

Stuart, D. *Hosea–Jonah.* Word Biblical Commentary 31. Waco, Tex.: Word Books, 1987. Note the bibliography, 424–431.

Wolff, H. W. *Obadiah and Jonah.* Translated by M. Kohl. Minneapolis: Augsburg Publishing House, 1976. Note the bibliography through 1976, 88–93.

Zlotowitz, M. *Yonah/Jonah: A New Translation with a Commentary Anthologized from Midrashic and Rabbinic Sources.* Brooklyn, N.Y.: Mesorah Publications, 1978.

2. Books and Monographs

Benoît, P., J. T. Milik, and R. de Vaux. *Les grottes de Murabba'ât.* Discoveries in the Judaean Desert, vol. 2. Oxford: Clarendon Press, 1961.

Cathcart, K. J., and R. P. Gordon. *The Targum of the Minor Prophets.* Aramaic Bible, vol. 14. Wilmington, Del.: Michael Glazier, 1989.

Charlesworth, J., ed. *The Old Testament Pseudepigrapha.* 2 vols. Garden City, N.Y.: Doubleday & Co., 1983, 1985.

Friedlander, G., ed. and trans. *Pirḳê de Rabbi Eliezer.* London: Kegan Paul, Trench, Trubner & Co.; New York: Bloch Publishing Co., 1916.

Jeremias, Joachim. *Heiligengräber in Jesu Umwelt.* Göttingen: Vandenhoeck & Ruprecht, 1958.

Jeremias, Jörg. *Die Reue Gottes.* Biblische Studien 65. Neukirchen-Vluyn: Neu-
kirchener Verlag, 1975.
LaCocque, A. and P.-E. *Jonah: A Psycho-Religious Approach to the Prophet.*
Columbia, S.C.: University of South Carolina Press, 1990.
Levine, E. *The Aramaic Version of Jonah.* Brooklyn, N.Y.: Sepher-Hermon Press,
1981[3].
Magonet, J. *Form and Meaning: Studies in Literary Techniques in the Book of
Jonah.* Sheffield: Almond Press, 1983[2].
Simon, M., and P. P. Levertoff, eds. *The Zohar.* Vol. 4. London: Soncino Press,
1934.
Steffen, U. *Jona und der Fisch: Der Mythos von Tod und Wiedergeburt.* Stuttgart:
Kreuz Verlag, 1985[2].
——. *Das Mysterium von Tod und Auferstehung: Formen und Wandlungen des
Jona-Motivs.* Göttingen: Vandenhoeck & Ruprecht, 1963.
Thackston, W. M., Jr. *The Tales of the Prophets of al-Kisa'i.* Boston: Twayne
Publishers, 1978.
Vanoni, G. *Das Buch Jona.* Arbeiten zu Text und Sprache im Alten Testament
7. St. Ottilien: EOS-Verlag, 1978.
Wolff, H. W. *Studien zum Jonabuch.* Biblische Studien 47. Neukirchen-Vluyn:
Neukirchener Verlag, 1965[2].
Wünsche, A. *Aus Israels Lehrhallen.* 3 vols. Hildesheim: Georg Olms, 1967.

3. Articles and Chapters

Bickerman, E. "Les deux erreurs du prophète Jonas." In *Studies in Jewish and
Christian History,* 33–71. Leiden: E. J. Brill, 1976.
Burrows, M. "The Literary Category of the Book of Jonah." In *Translating and
Understanding the Old Testament: Essays in Honor of Herbert Gordon May,*
edited by H. T. Frank and W. L. Reed, 80–107. Nashville: Abingdon Press, 1970.
Craig, K. "Jonah and the Reading Process." *JSOT* 47 (1990): 103–114.
Day, J. "Problems in the Interpretation of the Book of Jonah." In *In Quest of
the Past: Studies on Israelite Religion, Literature, and Prophetism,* edited by
A. S. van der Woude, 32–47. Kinderhook, N.Y.: E. J. Brill (U.S.A.), 1990.
Gese, H. "Jona ben Amittai und das Jonabuch." In *Alttestamentliche Studien,*
122–138. Tübingen: J. C. B. Mohr (Paul Siebeck), 1991.
Halpern, B., and R. E. Friedman, R. E. "Composition and Paronomasia in the
Book of Jonah." *HAR* 4 (1980): 79–92.
Komlos, O. "Jonah Legends." In *Etudes orientales à la mémoire de Paul Hirschler,*
41–61. Budapest: Allamositott, 1950.
Landes, G. "Linguistic Criteria and the Date of the Book of Jonah." In *Eretz-
Israel* (the Orlinsky volume), 16:147–170. 1982.
Limburg, J. "Jonah and the Whale Through the Eyes of Artists." *Bible Review*
6 (August 1990): 18–25.
Magonet, J. "Jonah, Book of." *Anchor Bible Dictionary.* Garden City, N.Y.:
Doubleday & Co., 1992.
Robinson, B. P. "Jonah's Qiqayon Plant." *ZAW* 97 (1985): 390–403.

Vanoni, G., U. Steffen, et al. "Jona als Typ unsterblich." *Bibel heute* 27 (1991, 1st quarter).

Weimar, P. "Jon 2, 1-11; Jonapsalm und Jonaerzählung." *BZ* 28 (1984): 43-68.

———. "Jon 4,5; Beobachtungen zur Entstehung der Jonaerzählung." *BN* 18 (1982): 86-109.

———. "Literarische Kritik und Literarkritik; Unzeitgemässe Beobachtungen zu Jon 1, 4-16." In *Künder des Wortes; Beiträge zur Theologie der Propheten. Festschrift J. Schreiner,* edited by L. Ruppert, P. Weimar, and E. Zenger, 217-235. Würzburg: Echter Verlag, 1982.

Zobel, H.-J. "Jonah/Jonabuch." *Theologische Realenzyklopädie,* 17:233-234. 1987.

INTRODUCTION

Jonah Among the Prophetic Books

It is not immediately apparent that the story of Jonah should be grouped with the prophetic writings of the Old Testament. Jonah is never called "prophet" in the book that bears his name. Since the Jonah material is a story *about* a prophet rather than a collection of prophetic sayings, it could have fit well in the books of Kings, where there are a number of stories about prophets. In fact, many phrases from Jonah find their closest biblical parallels in the narratives about Elijah and Elisha (1 Kings 17– 2 Kings 9).[1] An account involving a huge fish (and a small worm) would not have been out of place there, since these narratives in Kings already tell of encounters between prophets and lions (1 Kings 13:20–32; 20:35–36), bears (2 Kings 2:23–25), ravens (1 Kings 17:4–6), and a donkey (1 Kings 13:20–32). The Jonah material could have been placed after the reference to Jonah son of Amittai in 2 Kings 14:25.

Or one could imagine the book of Jonah as part of the third section of the Hebrew canon, the Writings. As a short narrative about a memorable figure from Israel's history, Jonah would also have fit well here, next to the books of Ruth and Esther.

Jonah might have taken its place alongside Tobit in the Apocrypha. That story starts and ends in Nineveh and in fact refers twice to Jonah's prophecy about the city (Tobit 14:4, 8, RSV).[2] One incident is especially interesting: Tobias camps on the banks of the Tigris and goes down to the river to wash himself. "A fish leaped up from the river and would have swallowed the young man," the story continues, but Tobias and the angel accompanying him end up eating the fish instead (Tobit 6:1–5, RSV).

1. The biblical canon, however, has located Jonah as one of the prophets in the Book of the Twelve. This collection has existed alongside the great books of Isaiah, Jeremiah, and Ezekiel at least since the time of the writing of Sirach in the second century B.C.:

---

[1] See pp. 29–30 below.

[2] For a comment on the text of Tobit, see p. 80 below.

May the bones of the Twelve Prophets
send forth new life from where they lie,
for they comforted the people of Jacob
and delivered them with confident hope.
(Sir. 49:10)

In both the Masoretic text and the Hebrew scroll of the twelve prophets found at Wadi Murabba'at near the Dead Sea,[3] Jonah is the fifth of the prophets in the collection: Hosea, Joel, Amos, Obadiah, Jonah, Micah, Nahum, Habakkuk, Zephaniah, Haggai, Zechariah, Malachi. In the Greek codices Vaticanus and Alexandrinus, Jonah is in sixth place. These Greek manuscripts begin the collection of the Twelve Prophets with Hosea, Amos, and Micah, linking these figures identified with the eighth century in their superscriptions, and then follow with Joel, Obadiah, and Jonah; the last six books follow the Hebrew order.[4]

2. In both the Hebrew and Greek manuscript traditions, the three longer prophetic books appear in chronological order according to their superscriptions: Isaiah, Jeremiah, and Ezekiel. The context of the Sirach quotation cited above reflects this same order, mentioning Isaiah (Sir. 48:22), Jeremiah (Sir. 49:6–7), and Ezekiel (Sir. 49:8) before the "Twelve Prophets" (Sir. 49:10).

A chronological factor has also been operative in the arrangement of the Book of the Twelve. If we begin by considering those six books which provide chronological data in their superscriptions, the order is:

Hosea/Amos (Uzziah/Jeroboam, eighth century; Hosea also lists Jotham, Ahaz, and Hezekiah in Judah)
Micah (Jotham, Ahaz, and Hezekiah, eighth century)
Zephaniah (Josiah, seventh century)
Haggai (second year of Darius, 520 B.C., sixth month)
Zechariah (second year of Darius, eighth month)

A second factor in the arrangement of these books appears to be catchword linkage. Joel and Amos are joined in this way. The beginning of Amos (1:2a) links up with a statement near the end of Joel (3:16a). The closing chapter of Joel speaks of a judgment of all the nations, including Tyre, Sidon, and the regions of Philistia (Joel 3:1–8); the opening chapter of Amos includes judgments pronounced upon Tyre (Amos 1:9–10) and the cities of Philistia (Amos 1:6–8). Finally, the last word of Joel is "in Zion"

---

[3] See p. 33 below.

[4] A listing of the twelve prophets in 2 Esd. 1:38–40, a segment from about A.D. 150, follows the Greek order. The order of the twelve prophets in the *Martyrdom and Ascension of Isaiah*, from the end of the first century A.D., differs from both the Hebrew and the Greek. See Appendix for both texts.

and the first saying in Amos begins, "Yahweh from Zion" (Amos 1:2). Another Joel-Amos link is found in Joel 3:18a and Amos 9:13b.

Amos also has thematic ties with Obadiah. Near the end of Amos is a saying concerning Edom (Amos 9:12), while Obadiah is introduced as a word from the Lord concerning Edom (Obad. 1).

Joel, Amos, and Obadiah are also linked with the common theme of the day of the Lord, in Joel 2:31; 3:14; Amos 5:18–20; and Obad. 15. These catchword and thematic links thus tie these three prophets together in the order Joel-Amos-Obadiah.

Since the superscriptions of both Hosea and Amos place them in the time of King Uzziah and King Jeroboam, the chronological factor could have put either one at the beginning of these twelve books. But if Amos had already been sandwiched between Joel and Obadiah at the time the final collection of the Twelve Prophets was being made, Hosea would have been given first position. Hosea may have been given initial position because it is longer than Amos and is in fact the longest book in the Twelve Prophets.

Some of the other books in this collection of twelve prophets have clear chronological indications, even though such information is not found in the superscription. Since Jonah son of Amittai is mentioned in 2 Kings 14:23–27 as a contemporary of King Jeroboam II, the book of Jonah fits with Hosea and Amos, who are also linked with Jeroboam. Probably because of its brevity, Jonah follows the lengthy Hosea and the Joel-Amos-Obadiah series. Jonah is placed before Micah because Micah's superscription dates the book after the time of Jeroboam.

Nahum announces the fall of Nineveh, which took place in 612 B.C.; if we assume that he prophesied shortly before that date, this book fits chronologically after Micah. Habakkuk speaks of the rise of the Chaldeans or neo-Babylonians (Hab. 1:6), which locates him just after 612 B.C., suggesting that the book follow Nahum. We are left with the book of Malachi, which assumes the existence of the second temple (Mal. 1:7, 10; 3:1) and thus follows chronologically upon Haggai and Zechariah.

3. Jonah's location in the context of the prophetic books in general and the Book of the Twelve in particular suggests some directions for the interpretation of the book.

First, Jonah is the only prophetic book that is primarily a story about a prophet. Prophetic books are made up of words from God to the people through the prophet, words from the prophet to God (prayer), and biographical or autobiographical material about the prophet. The Jonah book contains a brief word from God (3:4b) and a prayer (the bulk of Jonah 2), but it is mostly a story about the prophet. This unique feature must be taken into account if the book is to be rightly understood and is thus considered in the section that follows.

Second, the linking of Jonah with Hosea, Amos, and Micah in the Book of the Twelve indicates that Jonah ought to be understood as a story about a person from the eighth century B.C. Jonah's link with that time is also evident from his identification as "son of Amittai" (Jonah 1:1 and 2 Kings 14:23–27). Canonical context and the reference to 2 Kings both suggest that no matter when the story may have been written, we need to understand it in the context of the ancient Near Eastern world of the eighth century B.C., when Assyria was the rising world power and Nineveh was a great world city.

Third, in reading Jonah in the context of the prophetic books, we discover that Jonah is the only one of these prophets sent to proclaim a message in a foreign land. Other prophets delivered oracles concerning foreign nations (Amos 1–2; Obadiah; Nahum; Isaiah 13–23; Jeremiah 46–50; Ezekiel 25–32), but only Jonah is portrayed as walking down the streets of one of the major cities of the ancient world to deliver his message.

Finally, as we consider Jonah in the context of the biblical prophets we also discover that only Jonah needs to have his assignment from the Lord given to him a second time. The doubling of the Lord's directive suggests to the interpreter that this assignment to carry out a mission in Nineveh was important, very important indeed.

Jonah as Didactic Story

The book of Jonah contains a number of examples of shorter literary types. There are prayers (1:14; 2:2–9; 4:2–3, 8b), confessions of faith (1:9; 4:2b), and formulas introducing a word from the Lord (1:1; 3:1). There is a short prophetic saying (3:4b) and a royal proclamation (3:7–9).

But how should the book as a whole be categorized? Should it be described as a historical report, like 2 Kings 17:1–6? Or a fable, like Judg. 9:7–15? Is it to be understood as an allegory, such as that found in Ezekiel 17? Or should it be thought of as a parable, similar to the one in 2 Sam. 12:1–6? Is it a midrash (an imaginative exposition of a biblical text) on a text like Ex. 34:6 or Jer. 18:8, like the midrash [NRSV "commentary"] mentioned in 2 Chron. 24:27? Or like the story Jesus told in Luke 10:25–37, which may be considered a midrash on the question in 10:29?[5]

1. The book of Jonah begins with the Hebrew conjunction and verb *wayᵉhî,* often translated elsewhere as "and it happened" or "now it

---

[5] For a careful discussion of the issue, see Burrows, "The Literary Category of the Book of Jonah." He concludes that Jonah should be described as a satire.

happened." Eight other biblical books begin with this same *wayᵉhî*. In each instance that word introduces a narrative book (Joshua, Judges, Ruth, 1 Samuel, 2 Samuel, Esther, Nehemiah) or a narrative section of a book (Ezekiel). The King James Version translated seven of these eight occurrences as "and/now it came to pass" (all except 1 Samuel). The *wayᵉhî* at the beginning of the Jonah book thus suggests to a reader or hearer that a narrative — or story — is to follow.

The book of Jonah begins:

> Now the word of the LORD came (*wayᵉhî*) to Jonah son of Amittai, saying: "Get up, go to Nineveh." . . . But Jonah got up. . . . (Jonah 1:1–3)

The closest parallels to this beginning are found in the Elijah narratives in 1 Kings. The Elijah cycle is introduced:

> Now the word of the LORD came (*wayᵉhî*) to him, saying: "Go . . . ."
> So he went . . . . (1 Kings 17:2–5, my translation)

The same pattern is repeated a few verses later:

> Now the word of the LORD came (*wayᵉhî*) to him, saying: "Get up, go to Zarephath . . . ." So he got up and he went . . . . (1 Kings 17:8–10, my translation)

The same formula with a command is also found in 1 Kings 21:17 and 28; see also the similar formulation in 18:1.

This *wayᵉhî* formula in 1 Kings occurs in a section of the Old Testament that contains a high concentration of miracle stories connected with prophets, especially miracle stories involving nature: ravens bring food (1 Kings 17:1–8); bread and oil multiply (1 Kings 17:9–16); fire and rain appear (1 Kings 18); wind, an earthquake, and fire come (1 Kings 19:11–12); a lion kills a man (1 Kings 20:35–36); fire comes down (2 Kings 1:10, 12); the Jordan is parted, a whirlwind carries Elijah to heaven, water is purified, bears kill boys (2 Kings 2); oil is multiplied (2 Kings 4:1–7); stew is purified (2 Kings 4:38–41); bread is multiplied (2 Kings 4:42–44); and an axhead floats (2 Kings 6:1–7). The Jonah narrative, with its miraculous events involving the storm, the fish, the plant, the worm, and the wind, fits well with these materials.

What term should be used to describe the material in the book of Jonah? In consideration of these other examples, Jonah may be described as a story, just as one speaks of the stories of Ruth or Esther or stories about Joshua or Nehemiah or Elijah or Elisha. The advantage of the term "story" is that it is neutral regarding the question of historicity. One can speak of the story of the fall of Jerusalem in 587 B.C. or of the story of the arrival of Columbus in the New World in 1492. One can also refer to the story of the ewe lamb in 2 Samuel 12 or the story of the Good Samaritan in Luke 10, both of which are stories that were invented.

Jonah should be understood alongside the story about the trees told by Jotham (Judg. 9:7–15) or the story about the lamb that Nathan told David (2 Samuel 12) or the parables that Jesus told. None of these stories ever "happened," but each of them carried — and continues to carry — a powerful message. The book of Jonah may be described as a fictional story developed around a historical figure for didactic purposes.[6] This means that the size and species of the big fish (as well of the small worm) in the story may be left to the imagination. But the message of the story of Jonah ought to be taken as seriously as the message of the parable of the waiting father or the good Samaritan or any other part of the Bible. Considering Jonah in this way should not be understood as advocating a general approach to scripture that does not take history seriously.[7]

Claus Westermann has provided a helpful definition of a narrative or story: "A story narrates a series of events from a point of tension to the resolution of that tension."[8] This may be illustrated by considering some other biblical narratives that begin with *wayₑhî*. The tension driving a narrative may be put in the form of a question: "Who shall go up first for us against the Canaanites . . . ?" (Judg. 1:1). In 1 Samuel the tension is expressed in 1:2 which raises the questions: What will happen to Hannah? Will she have a child? In 2 Samuel the tension is introduced with the strange sight of a man with dirt on his head: What happened to him? Ruth 1:1–5 raises the question: How will these women survive? Esther 3 asks: Now

---

[6] Some consider Jonah as a historical account. Among recent commentators are G. F. Hasel, *Jonah, Messenger of the Eleventh Hour* (Mountain View, Calif.: Pacific Press Publishing Assn., 1976); G. Maier, *Der Prophet Jona* (Wuppertal: R. Brockhaus Verlag, 1976); and Stuart, *Hosea–Jonah*. See also D. J. Wiseman, "Jonah's Nineveh," *Tyndale Bulletin* 30 (1979): 29–51.

[7] I am in agreement with the comment of Brevard Childs: "By determining that the book of Jonah functions in its canonical context as a parable-like story the older impasse regarding the historicity of the story is by-passed as a theological issue. Because the book serves canonically in the role of an analogy, it is as theologically irrelevant to know its history as it is with the Parable of the Good Samaritan. In both instances historical features have been incorporated within the narrative, but this determination does not affect the canonical role which the book plays. . . . This is a judgment regarding the canonical function of Jonah and is not to be generalized into a principle that history is unimportant for the Bible" (*Introduction to the Old Testament as Scripture* [Philadelphia: Fortress Press, 1979], 426). Hans Walter Wolff speaks of a process of dehistoricizing (*Enthistorisierung*) in the book: Jonah becomes a type with which the reader or hearer identifies himself or herself; Nineveh has a "king," but no name is given; since Assyria is not mentioned, Nineveh remains a type of the big city; Tarshish is a symbol of a far-off place (*Studien,* 49).

[8] "Eine Erzählung dichtet ein Geschehen von einer Spannung zu einer Lösung" (C. Westermann, *Genesis 12–50* [Darmstadt: Wissenschaftliche Buchgesellschaft, 1975], p. 33, my translation).

that the king has been tricked into ordering the execution of all Jews, what will happen to Mordecai and Esther and the rest of their people?

In each of these *wayehî* texts outside Jonah, the narrative is introduced with the establishing of a tension that requires resolution. The tension introduced in Jonah 1:1-3 may be expressed with two questions: What will happen to a prophet who so blatantly disobeys the Lord? What will happen to the wicked city of Nineveh?

2. Can the literary category "story" as applied to Jonah be more precisely defined? One is struck by the fact that this short book contains fourteen *questions.*[9] In the first part of the story, all of the questions are directed at Jonah. The captain questions him (1:6). The sailors interrogate him with seven questions (1:8, 10, 11). In the psalm, Jonah asks a question of the Lord (2:4). The king of Nineveh asks a rhetorical question (3:9). In the final chapter, Jonah puts an angry question to the Lord (4:2) and the Lord/God addresses three questions to Jonah (4:4, 9, 11).

If a story is skillfully told, the storyteller can use questions to put each listener in the place of the one being questioned. The eight questions in Jonah 1 thus lead the listener to put himself or herself in the role of Jonah. Hans Walter Wolff comments on the fact that Jonah is never called "prophet" in the book: "In the course of the narrative Jonah is more the one who is questioned than the one who preaches." What does it mean for understanding the story, if the hearer or reader takes the place of Jonah? Wolff points to Jonah's own answer in 1:9: "I am a Hebrew." The Jonah story is thus addressed to each individual Israelite or to each individual who is a part of the people of God.[10] The book concludes with a series of three questions directed at Jonah/the listener and in fact ends with just such a question. Some eleven questions are directed to Jonah/the hearer in the course of the story, thus placing the listener in the role of Jonah in the story and leaving the listener with the Lord's final question still ringing in his or her ears.[11]

---

[9] Wolff (*Studien,* 52-53) points out that Jonah is often brought into the scene of action by means of questions: Jonah 1:6, 8, 11; 4:4, 9, 11.

[10] Wolff, *Studien,* 72 (my translation).

[11] Wolff's commments are again illuminating: "In this way [Jonah] is related to the parable, as we know it in the Old Testament in the form of Isaiah's song about the friend and his vineyard (5:1-7) and in Nathan's parable of the poor man's lamb (2 Sam. 12:1-7). The special features of the Jonah novelle include the way it is structured into scenes, the choice of a historical figure for its 'hero,' and the refusal to spell out the meaning of the story in the manner of 2 Sam. 12:7 ('You are the Jonah!') or Isa. 5:7 ('The house of Israel is Jonah, and the obstinate ones are the people of Judah'). Thus the Jonah story hides the didactic element. To be sure, the reader of the Jonah story is left with a question that is put to him or her; but this question remains in the realm of the novelle as a question addressed to Jonah" (*Studien,* 53-54, my translation).

What sort of literature is especially marked by the use of questions? One thinks immediately of the questions in Proverbs (1:22; 5:16, 20; 6:9, 27, 28, 30; etc.) or in Ecclesiastes (1:10; 2:2, 15, 19, 22, 25; 3:9, 21; 4:8, 11; etc.) or in Job (2:9, 10; 3:11, 12, 16, 20–22, 23; etc.). The use of questions is especially characteristic of wisdom literature, the aim of which is to instruct.

The frequent use of questions suggests that the book of Jonah has a didactic aim. Another observation points in the same direction. The book contains a number of statements that are compact, almost dogmatic in nature, each of which speaks about the Lord/God: Jonah's confession of faith in 1:9, carefully positioned in the center of scene II; the third-person statements about the Lord in 2:2a, 7a, 9b and the declaration in 2:8; the confession of faith in 4:2b.

The use of questions and these explicitly theological declarations suggest that Jonah be categorized as a *didactic story*.[12] Appropriate interpretive questions will be: What is the instructional aim of the story as a whole? What does this portion of the story intend to teach? The interpreter will want to pay special attention to the questions in the story, especially to the final question.

3. Jonah is a didactic story that was designed to be heard. Before the invention of the printing press and the wide distribution of printed texts, most people who encountered Jonah heard the story as it was read or told before a gathered community. We cannot recapture the inflection of the storyteller's voice, the varied tempos, the expression on the face, the gestures or the pauses as the story was read or told. We can, however, note a number of characteristics of the Jonah story that suggest it was intended to be read or told aloud.

The use of *direct discourse* enlivens a story by making it possible for the reader or storyteller to take the role of the various characters in the story. The book of Jonah is divided into forty-eight sentences or verses. Of these, thirty-two, or two-thirds, contain at least some direct discourse. If we consider the words of the book, we discover that 346 of the 688 words, or very close to one half, are used in direct discourse. The speakers are the Lord (1:2; 3:2; 4:4, 9, 10, 11); the captain (1:6); the sailors (1:7, 8, 10, 11, 14); Jonah (1:9, 12; 2:2–9; 3:4; 4:2–3, 8–9; and the king (3:7–9). The author has constructed these speeches with care: in the last chapter of the book, the speeches of Jonah (4:2–3) and of the Lord (4:10–11) are exactly balanced, each consisting of thirty-nine words.[13]

---

[12] Wolff comments on the subtle nature of the instruction in the book: "The didactic element is totally taken up into the form of the story. No obvious 'teaching' ever appears. The reader is caught up in the story rather than catechized" (*Studien*, 56, my translation).

[13] Magonet, *Form*, 56.

The *repetition* of words in written material quickly becomes monotonous, but in oral discourse the speaker can play upon the repeated word or words, varying pitch, volume, and tempo for dramatic effect. In general, repetition serves to emphasize. For example, the repetition of the second half of each verse in Psalm 136 when read silently becomes boring; when read aloud, however, the repeated phrases can develop rhetorical power. The root *gdl,* "big, great," occurs fourteen times in the Jonah book. The effect of hearing this repeated word gives the story a naive, almost childlike quality which is apparent if it is translated the same way each time. Again, such repetition could be allowed in oral material but not in written: big city (1:2), big wind, big storm (1:4), big fear (1:10), big storm (1:12), big fear (1:16), big fish (1:17), big city (3:2), big city (3:3), from the biggest (3:5), king and his "big ones" (3:7), big anger (4:1), big gladness (4:6), big city (4:11). Another example is the word translated "hurl": the Lord hurled a big wind onto the sea (1:4), the sailors hurl the cargo into the sea (1:5), Jonah suggests they hurl him into the sea (1:12) and they do hurl him (1:15). Or, notice the way in which the verb "go down" traces the descent of Jonah: he went down to Joppa (1:3), he went down into the ship (1:3), went down into the hold (1:5), and finally went down to the bottom of the mountains (2:6). These are just a few examples; others can be added.[14]

A special variation of repetition is the *extension* or *diminution* of phrases. Again, such repetitions are most effective when the story is heard rather than read silently. In Jonah 1, the increasing intensity of the storm is described by the increasing length of each description (1:4, 11, 13). Another series of "growing phrases" describes the increasing fear of the sailors (1:5, 10, 16). The winding down of the storm is effectively described in 1:16 with three clauses that become progressively shorter.[15]

In addition to repetition, another way of providing emphasis in Hebrew is to employ *subject-verb word order* rather than the usual verb-subject order; examples are listed with the comments on 1:4.

Finally, we note some rhetorical/literary devices employed. *Personification* attributes human characteristics to a nonhuman subject: "the ship threatened [lit. "thought"] to break up" (1:4); also, "the sea . . . raging" (1:15). *Merismus* names the extremes to denote the entire class: sea and dry land (1:9); days and nights (1:17); greatest/least (3:5); human being/ animal (3:7, 8); persons/animals (4:11). As an example of *metaphor,* note "heart of the sea" in 2:3.

---

[14] See the commentary on 1:2 for the play on *qārā',* "call"; and on 3:6 for the play on *dbr,* or on 4:1 for the play on *rā'āh.* Note also Halpern and Friedman, 79–82; and Magonet, *Form,* ch. 1.

[15] See the commentary on these passages; cf. Magonet, *Form,* 31–32.

Jonah has been described as a "desk job,"[16] and in its final form, of course, the book was written down. The careful use of words and the sophisticated construction of the whole indicate that much intellectual work has gone into its production. The story of Jonah was heard by a listening community for many more centuries than it has been available in written form. Its careful design was first intended to communicate through the ear rather than the eye. In order to experience the story as it was first intended to be experienced, it should be read aloud. In addition to watching for the techniques of the writer, the interpreter should listen for the devices of the speaker and storyteller.

4. The book of Jonah may be divided into seven scenes. The story begins with an account of Jonah's call and his reaction (1:1–3). Scene II takes place on board ship in the midst of a storm at sea (1:4–16). The setting for scene III is inside the great fish (1:17–2:10). Scene IV gives Jonah his assignment one more time (3:1–3a). Scene V takes place in Nineveh (3:3b–10) and scene VI consists of Jonah's prayer, prayed in Nineveh (4:1–3). The final scene takes place outside the city, beginning and ending with the Lord putting questions to the prophet (4:4–11).[17]

Date, Composition, and Text

The historical setting for the story told in the book of Jonah is clear. The reference to "Jonah son of Amittai" identifies Jonah with the prophet of 2 Kings 14:25 who worked during the days of Jeroboam II (786–746 B.C.). The matter of the time of the composition of the story, however, is far from clear. The chronological boundaries are the eighth and second centuries B.C., since Sirach assumes the existence of Jonah among the Twelve Prophets (Sir. 49:10).[18]

---

[16] "Schreibtischarbeit" (Vanoni, 153).

[17] The MT places a *pe* for *petuḥah* (open paragraph) after 2:10 [Heb. 2:11], indicating that the major break in the story comes at the end of ch. 2. The MT places a *samech* for *setumah* (closed paragraph) after 2:9 [2:10] and 4:3, indicating lesser breaks at these points. The Dead Sea Scroll also indicates these points of division, leaving a vacant line between 2:9 and 2:10 [2:10 and 2:11], a gap of the length of two or three words after 2:10 [2:11], and a vacant line and a half after 4:3; see DJD, 2:192. The analysis of the structure of the book in this commentary takes into account these ancient clues to the book's divisions.

[18] The wide range of current scholarly opinion suggests that settling the issue of the date for the composition of Jonah is not likely: eighth century B.C. (Hasel, 95–98, and Maier, 26 [see p. 24 n. 6 above]); sixth century (Landes, *IDBSup,* 490; and idem, "Linguistic Criteria," 163); sixth to fourth century (Magonet, *ABD*); sixth to third century (Rudolph, 330); fifth century, between 475 and 450 (Fretheim, 34–37); fifth or fourth century (Allen, 188); first half of fourth century (Gese, 123–124); late fourth century (Wolff, *Obadiah and Jonah,* 78). Sasson (pp. 20–28) discusses the matter at length, concluding that "a final editing or composing of Jonah took place during the exilic, but more likely during the postexilic period. At the

Is it possible to determine more precisely when the book was written? Is the book a unity, or is it made up of several redactional layers? Finally, what about the textual sources for the Jonah story?

1. In considering the date for the composition of the book, we begin with some linguistic observations. A number of Hebrew words or expressions in Jonah occur elsewhere mainly (or exclusively) in writings that are clearly postexilic. The relative particle *še*, "who, which," with compound forms *bešellemî, bešellî,* occurs in Jonah 1:7, 12; 4:10. While there are examples of *še* in preexilic texts, the great majority are found in postexilic writings.[19] The verb *mānāh,* "appoint," occurs in Jonah 1:17 [2:1]; 4:6, 7, 8. There are ten more occurrences of the verb and its Aramaic cognate with this sense in the Old Testament, eight of these in clearly postexilic contexts; Hebrew: 1 Chron. 9:29; Dan. 1:5, 10, 11; Aramaic: Dan. 2:24, 49; 3:12; Ezra 7:25 (the others are Ps. 61:7 [8] and Job 7:3). The noun *ribbô,* meaning ten thousand, occurs in 4:11 as a component of the number 120,000. The Hebrew *ribbô* or *ribbô'* is a shorter synonym of *rebābāh;* other occurrences are all in postexilic texts: 1 Chron. 29:7; Ezra 2:64 = Neh. 7:66, 71; plural in Neh. 7:70; Ezra 2:69 and Dan. 11:12. The expression "the LORD, the God of heaven" (Jonah 1:9) also occurs in Gen. 24:7 (cf. 24:3, "heaven and earth") and then in the postexilic texts Ezra 1:2; 2 Chron. 36:23; Neh. 1:5. The phrase "the God of heaven" occurs in Ps. 136:26 and then often in postexilic literature: Neh. 1:4; 2:4; the Aramaic equivalent in Ezra 5:11, 12; 6:9, 10; 7:12, 21, 23 (twice); Dan. 2:18, 19, 37, 44.

There are also a few words or constructions that appear only in Jonah in the Hebrew part of the Bible but that do also occur in (postexilic) Aramaic texts. The verb *yit'aššēt,* "give a thought to," occurs only in Jonah 1:6 and in its Aramaic cognate form in Dan. 6:4. The noun *ta'am,* "decree," in Jonah 3:7 has this sense only here in the Hebrew Bible; its Aramaic cognate with this meaning occurs often (Ezra 4:19, 21 twice; 5:3, 9, 13, 17; 6:1, 3, 8, 11, 12, 14; 7:13, 21, 23; Dan. 3:10, 29; 4:6 [3]; 6:26 [27]).

These connections with postexilic vocabulary do not prove that Jonah was composed in the postexilic period, but the evidence surely points in that direction.[20]

Second, Jonah contains a number of words or expressions that connect with other biblical materials. We have already noted the connection between the opening words of the Jonah book and similar expressions in the Elijah/

---

same time, however, I acknowledge how little this admission contributes to a fuller understanding of this particular book" (p. 27).

[19] BDB comments, "In usage limited to late Heb., and passages with N. Palest. colouring," and lists occurrences (pp. 979–980).

[20] On the matter of language and dating, see the comments of Day, 34–36.

Elisha materials.[21] There are further points of contact between Jonah and
these materials. It is reported of Elijah, "and he asked that he might die,
saying . . ." (1 Kings 19:4); the identical words appear in Jonah 4:8. The
1 Kings passage continues with, "now, O Lord, take away my life"; those
same words appear in Jonah 4:3. It is next reported of Elijah, "and he
lay down" (19:5); the same verb occurs in Jonah 1:5. In addition to these
verbal points of contact, both Jonah and the Elijah materials contain an
unusual number of nature miracles.[22] Finally, Elijah, like Jonah, is sent
on a mission to a foreign land (1 Kings 17:8–24).

Other biblical parallels may be noted briefly. Jonah's prayer in ch. 2 is
made up of traditional language from the psalms (see the commentary),
but these psalms provide no certain clues for dating. Jonah 3:9 and Joel
2:13 are partially identical (see the commentary), but since the date for
Joel is uncertain, and since it is not clear who borrowed from whom, these
texts do not help in dating Jonah.

Finally, a thematic consideration may be taken into account. In a public
proclamation the king of Nineveh says:

> "Who knows? God may turn and change his mind and turn from the
> heat of his anger and we will not die." And God saw what they did,
> how they turned from their evil ways; and God changed his mind about
> the evil which he said he would do against them, and he did not do it.
> (Jonah 3:9–10)

This statement reads like an illustration of the principle set forth in Jer.
18:7–8; words common to Jonah and Jeremiah are italicized:

> If at any time I declare concerning a nation or a kingdom, that I will
> pluck up and break down and destroy it, and if that nation, concerning
> which I have spoken, *turns* from its *evil,* I will change my mind *about
> the evil* that I intended *to do to* it. (Jer. 18:7–8, RSV adapted)

Again, see Jer. 26:3; common vocabulary is italicized:

> It may be they will listen, *and every one turn from his evil way,* that
> I may *change my mind* about *the evil which* I intend to do to them
> because of their evil doings. (Jer. 26:3, RSV adapted)[23]

Jonah's report of God's change of mind thus illustrates what Jeremiah had
spoken about in 609 B.C., just before Jerusalem's fall. None of these
linguistic, literary, or thematic considerations is decisive for settling the
matter of the date of the composition of Jonah. Taken together, however,

---

[21] See p. 23 above.
[22] See p. 23 above.
[23] See also Jer. 26:13, 19.

they point to a time after Jeremiah and after the composition of Deuteronomy-2 Kings, a time in the late exilic or the postexilic period.

In some cases, the superscription of a prophetic book points to a particular time period, as if to suggest that the first step in understanding the prophet is to understand the time (Isa. 1:1; Hos. 1:1; Amos 1:1; etc.). The editor of Jonah did not provide such information. The one chronological clue is the reference to "Jonah son of Amittai," about whom the hearers and readers of the story of Jonah would have known from the report in 2 Kings 14.[24]

Since determining the date for the composition of Jonah is such an elusive and probably impossible task, we may observe that perhaps setting such a date is after all not essential for understanding the book. Gerhard von Rad once wrote in connection with this issue, "It is best not to let conjecture about the contemporary causes of the book cloud our interpretation of it."[25]

2. What about the composition of the Jonah book? Was the prayer in Jonah 2 inserted into the story at a later stage?[26] If so, what would have

---

[24] See the commentary on Jonah 1:1.

[25] *Old Testament Theology,* 2:291–292; cf. also the comment of Sasson in note 1 above.

[26] So Rudolph, 347ff., and Wolff, *Obadiah and Jonah,* 78–79; Weimar (pp. 67–68) understands the incorporation of the Jonah psalm as a part of the second redactional layer of the book. Vanoni's argument for the secondary insertion of the prayer is especially extensive and may be taken as representative. He concludes (p. 35) that "a later interpolater" inserted the psalm in order to reinterpret the negative image of Jonah. Among his arguments: (1) The psalm is not linked to the prose section by common phrases or groups of words (Vanoni, 10). If, however, the psalm is made up of traditional phrases, one would not expect the same vocabulary as the narrative. Moreover, there are vocabulary links with words of thematic significance: "went down" of 2:6 [7] and 1:3, 5 (twice); "called" of 2:2 [3] and 1:6, 14; in addition: "sea" of 2:3 [4] is found eleven times in the narrative, though in the singular, while this is in the plural; three key words in this prayer also occur in the prayer of 4:2–3: *ḥayyîm* ("life") in 2:6 [7] and 4:3, 8; *nepeš* in 2:5 [6] ("me") and 2:7 [8] ("soul") in 4:3; and *ḥesed* ("love, steadfast love") in 2:8 [9] and 4:2; cf. the comments of Allen (p. 199 n. 108); "offer" and "vow" of 2:9 [10] and 1:16. (2) Mention of "thy holy temple" does not fit with a Jonah from the Northern Kingdom; we assume, however, that the story was written down long after the fall of the Northern Kingdom and the audience would understand this poetic license (contra his note 67, p. 15). (3) The prayer is a prayer of thanksgiving (*tôdāh*) but is introduced as a lament; but 1 Sam. 2:1 uses the same introduction for a thanksgiving, as Vanoni recognizes. (4) Ch. 2:6 [7] speaks of deliverance when Jonah is still in the fish (2:10 [11]); but the fish had delivered Jonah from death and, again, Vanoni is demanding more precision of poetry and story than can be expected. (5) Ch. 2:8 [9] does not square with the positive picture of the sailors; true, but this statement is aimed at the listening congregation. In sum, Vanoni (and others who list such "tensions" between the psalm and the narrative) demands a kind of mechanical correlation between psalm and narrative that is not to be expected in poetry and story. And if these tensions are so great, why should a redactor have allowed them? Cf. Gese, 136.

been the motivation for such an insertion?[27] Or has Jonah's prayer been
an integral part of the book from the beginning?[28]

In the first place, there are no decisive reasons for excising the psalm
from its present context. It has been argued that a psalm giving thanks
would be out of place in Jonah's situation; the huge fish, however, has
saved Jonah from drowning. Or, that such a prayer of thanks would be
out of character for the rebellious (1:1-3), irresponsible (1:5-6), and
recalcitrant (4:1-3) prophet; such an objection attempts to psychoanalyze
the prophet to a degree scarcely appropriate to the available evidence, and
alternations of rebellion and praise to God may be found throughout the
Psalter (Psalm 22). Are the differences in language between the psalm and
the narrative such that a different author is required? Jonah is clearly
quoting traditional material from the psalms,[29] as is also the case in 4:2,
and linguistic connections between the psalm and the narrative do exist.[30]

One might add that it is not necessary to prove that the psalm is part
of the original book of Jonah; the burden of proof is on the side of those
arguing in the other direction.

Second, the psalm is such an essential part of the narrative that it is
difficult to imagine a version of the Jonah story without it. Key words from
the narrative are picked up in the psalm: the reporting of the "going down"
of Jonah (1:3 twice, 5) reaches its deepest point as Jonah goes down "to
the bottom of the mountains" (2:6); when Jonah says "I called to the LORD"
(2:2), he is finally doing what the captain had asked him to do days before
(1:6), and what the sailors had done before throwing him overboard (1:14).

A story moving directly from 1:17 to 2:10, without the psalm, would
cut out the experience of near-death and deliverance that is here expressed,
reducing the monstrous fish to a means of transportation.[31] H. Gese writes:

> If one leaves the psalm in place as an original part of the narrative, then
> Jonah's experience of deliverance from death comes to expression with
> all the fullness and depth of Israel's psalm tradition. This experience
> does not eliminate the destiny of death but on the contrary intensifies
> it and makes God's act of deliverance from death all the more a victory
> over death. This experience which Jonah has with his God should be

---

[27] Additions to the Book of Esther, e.g., which includes a number of prayers and references
to God, was added to the canonical book at a later stage to give the book a more theological
slant, since Esther makes no mention of God.

[28] So Magonet, *Form,* ch. 2; and Gese, 136-138; note also the list of unifying features
given by Sasson, 19-20. See also Craig (pp. 103-114), who argues for the prayer as "part
of a major structural pattern in the book."

[29] See the commentary below.

[30] See n. 26 above.

[31] See the comments of Gese, 136-137.

set alongside the confession of the comprehensive mercy of God (beyond all partiality) to which God leads Jonah in chapter 4.[32]

In sum, there are no compelling reasons for considering the psalm as a later addition to Jonah and, in fact, it plays an essential role in the development of the narrative.

3. The translation in this commentary is based on the Masoretic text as represented by Codex Leningradensis, dated A.D. 1008 and printed in the *Biblia Hebraica Stuttgartensia*. A glance at the footnotes to Jonah in *BHS* reveals that textual problems are few; the commentary deals with those noted in *BHS* with the exception of minor matters of punctuation.

A partially complete Hebrew text of Jonah was discovered at Wadi Murabba'at in the Dead Sea area in March of 1955 and was published in 1961 as *Les grottes de Murabba'ât,* vol. 2 of Discoveries in the Judaean Desert.[33] Comparison of this text which dates from the second century A.D. with the Masoretic text of the Leningrad Codex reveals no significant textual variations.[34] The book of Jonah begins a new column in the scroll. Three lines are left blank after Jonah and before Micah. Within the text itself are spaces that correspond with the paragraph markings in the Masoretic text.[35]

Along with the rest of the Hebrew Bible, Jonah was translated into Greek in the third century B.C. When this commentary refers to the Greek or Septuagint, the edition of J. Ziegler has been used.[36]

The Targums are translations/paraphrases of the Hebrew scripture into Aramaic. *The Aramaic Bible,* vol. 14: *The Targum of the Minor Prophets,* ed. K. J. Cathcart and R. P. Gordon, provides a fresh translation of material dating "after 70 A.D."[37] without, however, reproducing the Aramaic text. The edition of E. Levine, *The Aramaic Version of Jonah,* offers the Aramaic text, translation, and commentary.

Theological Themes

What does the book of Jonah say about God? The theology informing the book comes to explicit expression in two statements of Jonah that

---

[32] Ibid., 137 (my translation).

[33] Ed. Benoît, Milik, and de Vaux: *Texte,* 183–184 and 190–192; *Planches,* photographs 60, 61. See also E. Würthwein, *The Text of the Old Testament,* trans. E. F. Rhodes (Grand Rapids: Wm. B. Eerdmans Publishing Co., 1979), 152–153.

[34] Benoît lists five minor differences (pp. 183–184).

[35] See p. 28 n. 17 above.

[36] *Septuaginta. Vetus Testamentum Graecum,* vol. 13: *Duodecim prophetae* (Göttingen: Vandenhoeck & Ruprecht, 1967²). For comments on the the Greek translation of Jonah, see L. Perkins, "The Septuagint of Jonah: Aspects of Literary Analysis Applied to Biblical Translation," *BIOSCS* 20 (1987): 43–45.

[37] Cathcart and Gordon, 16–18.

articulate traditional teaching about God (1:9; 4:2), a saying about idols (2:8), and in a number of declarations about the Lord in Jonah's prayer (2:2a, 7a, 9b). What is said about God in these statements should then be understood in the context of the Jonah story as a whole.

1. The book of Jonah asserts that *God has created, controls, and cares for the natural world.* Jonah's confession at the midpoint of the storm scene in 1:9 speaks of the Lord God's work of making the sea and the dry land, that is, of making all that exists. Almost in the manner of a first-article confession of faith, this statement places the Jonah book in the mainstream of the Old Testament's traditions about God as creator (Gen. 1:9–10; Ps. 95:5). If anything is clear about the notion of God informing this book, it is that God has not retired from the scene after creating the heavens and the earth. God controls the macro and the micro creatures and the forces of nature. The action of the story begins with the Lord hurling a great wind upon the vast sea (1:4) and ends as the Lord again sends a wind, this time directed at Jonah (4:8). The Lord appoints a huge fish (1:17 [2:1]), but also a tiny worm and a plant (4:6–7).

God's care for the creatures of nature is poignantly expressed in the last words of the book, "and also many animals." The animals too had taken part in Nineveh's repentance (3:7–8). The final words of the story of Jonah are a reminder that this planet with its seas and its dry land does not exist only for the sake of the hundreds of thousands, the millions of human beings who populate it. God is concerned that the animals find their rightful place as well.

2. Alongside these assertions of God's creating and sustaining work in nature, Jonah's prayer in ch. 2 testifies that *God rescues those who call upon him in trouble.* Jonah, having been rescued by the great fish, now tells about his experience. Three statements speak *about* the Lord's saving activity and are thus intended as theological witness to a listening congregation: "I called to the LORD out of my distress, and he answered me. . . . As my life was slipping away, I remembered the LORD. . . . Deliverance is from the LORD" (2:2a, 7a, 9b). Taken together, these words of witness speak comfort to those in the listening community who are experiencing distress, whose lives are slipping away, who yearn for release. Jonah had experienced a dramatic deliverance from death. Here he tells others about that experience and speaks of the God who rescues.

3. The book of Jonah testifies that *God cares about all the people of the earth.* Jonah's creedlike statement in 4:2b is a typical biblical expression of God's love for the people Israel (Ex. 34:6–7; Ps. 145:8; Joel 2:13; etc.). The only Israelite in this entire story is Jonah. God's love for Israel is illustrated in the Lord's compassion, patience, and love in dealing with this prophet! If the story had ended with 1:16, the point would have been

clear: Do not try to run away from the Lord! The Lord, however, continued to work with Jonah, rescuing him, giving him another chance, putting up with his petulance, patiently trying to instruct him. The point is clear: like a parent's love for a child, even a child who runs away, God's love for one of God's own people never gives up (Hosea 11).

However, these traditional attributes of God function in a fresh and non-traditional way in Jonah 4:2. God is described as compassionate and merciful, slow to anger, and filled with steadfast love — this time not toward the people of Israel but toward the people of Nineveh! God loves Israel, the people of God, but God also cares about the Ninevites, the people of the world. The story begins with God's decision to send a prophet to this huge but wicked city and ends with God's declaration of concern for its people and even for the animals that live there.

One cannot miss the positive portrayal of the non-Israelites, the "people of the world" in the story. The sailors along with their captain are men of piety and action (1:5–6), decent human beings (1:12–14) who are eager to do the right thing in the eyes of a God about whom they have heard little (1:14). They finally come to worship that God (1:16). After only a few words from the prophet Jonah about the corrupt state of their city, the people of Nineveh and their king, even their animals, all engage in sincere acts of repentance and turn their life-styles around (Jonah 3).

4. The story of Jonah makes clear that *God may change his mind about punishing.* When King Darius signed a decree, it could not be changed, even if the king himself wanted to grant amnesty (Dan. 6:8–15). God is not bound by any legal documents or pronouncements, even pronouncements God himself has made! When a people repent, God may call off an announced disaster, even a disaster announced by a prophet. Will God always do this? The king of Nineveh is a good enough theologian to respond, "Who knows?" (cf. Joel 2:14). The story of Jonah illustrates the saying of Jeremiah about the potter and the clay (Jer. 18:6–8).

5. The book of Jonah assumes that *the Lord is the only true God.* The author of the story is aware of religious pluralism, describing the piety (1:5–6) and practices (1:7) of the non-Israelite sailors without judgment or comment. The sailors, however, are not left to try to find the true God through their own religions but become worshipers of the Lord of Israel. The people of Nineveh respond positively to the message of the Lord's prophet.

The remaining didactic statement in Jonah's prayer gives further expression to this theme. With the declaration that "those who worship worthless idols abandon the one who loves them" in 2:8, the book makes clear that Yahweh, the Lord, is the only true God (cf. Ps. 31:6; Isa. 44:9–20; 45:5–6). The fact that this statement speaks about those who "abandon the one who has shown them steadfast love" suggests that slipping over into the worship of other gods must have been a real temptation for those first hearers of the Jonah story.

6. The story of Jonah indicates that *those who experience the Lord's deliverance are invited to respond in thanksgiving, witness, and praise.* There is a pattern in this story. The sailors are in distress, are delivered, and then respond by worshiping the Lord. Jonah is drowning, is delivered, and responds with word of witness and praise and with acts of worship. The story of Jonah not only portrays the God who creates, sustains, and delivers but also provides a model for the response of those who have experienced the Lord's blessing and deliverance. The story invites both the people of God and the peoples of the world to join in with the song of praise emerging from the belly of the great fish.

Approach and Suggestions for Using the Commentary

The division of the Jonah book into seven scenes is based on the content of the book as well as on clues in the traditional Hebrew text.[38] The discussion of each scene begins with a short description of the structure of the scene. Following this is a translation from the Hebrew with textual notes where appropriate. With one exception (2:4 [5]), the Masoretic text has been followed.

The comments that follow examine the words of the book in a series of increasingly wider contexts: the scene, the book, the Book of the Twelve, the Old and New Testaments.

A final section reflects on what the scene as a whole says about God, about God and people and the world of our own time. Especially helpful at this point have been the words and works of other interpreters of Jonah, including not only theologians but also artists, poets, and novelists.

The Appendix gathers a sampling of interpretations of Jonah in Judaism, Christianity, and Islam. Insights from these materials have been incorporated into the commentary. These works, many of which are not easily accessible, are cited in their entirety or in larger segments, so that the reader can use them on their own and make independent judgments about them.

---

[38] See p. 28 above.

COMMENTARY

The Runaway
1:1–3

The story gets off to a fast start. This first scene introduces the characters (the Lord, Jonah, the people of Nineveh, the sailors), gives the locations (Nineveh, Tarshish, Joppa, the ship), sets the tension for the story (What will happen to Jonah and to Nineveh?), and starts the action, as Jonah attempts to run away from the Lord. The tripling of "Tarshish" and the doubling of "Tarshish, away from the presence of the LORD" in v. 3 highlight the point of the scene.

> **1:1 Now the word of the LORD came to Jonah son of Amittai, saying: 2 "Get up, go to Nineveh, that great city, and preach¹ against it; for their wickedness has come before me." 3 But Jonah got up to run away to Tarshish, away from the presence of the LORD. So he went down to Joppa and found a ship going to Tarshish and paid its fare and went down into it to go with them to Tarshish, away from the presence of the LORD.**

[1:1] The first word in the book of Jonah in Hebrew is *way^ehî*, "and it happened," here translated, "Now . . . came." This is the typical biblical introduction to a narrative; the books of Joshua, Judges, Ruth, 1 and 2 Samuel, Esther, Nehemiah (1:1b), and Ezekiel (which opens with a narrative section) all begin in this way. This opening *way^ehî* is a signal that what follows will be a narrative, a story.²

These opening words make up a formula that is typical in the Deuteronomic History. The same expression is found in 1 Sam. 15:10 (Samuel); 2 Sam. 7:4 (Nathan); 1 Kings 6:11 (Solomon); 12:22 ("word of God," Shemaiah); 13:20 (the prophet); and 16:1 (Jehu). The formula occurs

---

¹ The verb *qārā'* is here translated "preach." The verb is used frequently in Jonah and has been translated a variety of ways in this commentary: 1:2, "preach"; 1:6, "call"; 1:14, "cried"; 2:2, "called"; 3:2, 4, 5, "proclaim," with the cognate accusative noun "proclamation" in 3:2; 3:8, "cry."

² See pp. 22–25 above.

frequently in the Elijah stories (1 Kings 17:2, 8; 21:17, 28; cf. 18:1). Reminiscences of the Elijah materials are especially frequent in Jonah.[3]

"Jonah" is the Hebrew word for "dove" (Gen. 8:8–12; S. of Sol. 1:15; 4:1; etc.). Since names taken from animals are not unusual in Hebrew,[4] there need not be any special significance to the name; in Hos. 7:11 a dove symbolizes Israel.

"Jonah son of Amittai" identifies the main character of this book with the prophet mentioned in 2 Kings 14:25.[5] That prophet would have been a familiar figure to the first hearers and readers of this biblical book. The Deuteronomic historian mentions Jonah in a report on the accomplishments of King Jeroboam (786–746 B.C.):

> He restored the border of Israel from Lebo-hamath as far as the Sea of the Arabah, according to the word of the LORD, the God of Israel, which he spoke by the hand of his servant Jonah son of Amittai, the prophet, who was from Gath-hepher. (2 Kings 14:25, my translation)

Jeroboam changed the map of Israel, extending the northern border to Lebo-hamath (the entrance of Hamath, south of Kadesh) and the southern border to the Dead Sea. This expansionist policy was made possible through two human instruments. The Lord *spoke* "by the hand of his servant Jonah son of Amittai," which meant that the prophet encouraged and advised the king, and the Lord *saved* "by the hand of Jeroboam son of Joash," referring to the king's activities on the battlefield (2 Kings 14:27).[6]

The biblical historian says that Jonah gave the king theological counsel on political and military matters, probably in the manner of the prophets of salvation described in 1 Kings 20:13–21 and 20:28–30. Since Jonah's counsel proved correct and effective, one may assume that Jonah son of Amittai enjoyed a good reputation in his homeland. The identification of Jonah as "the prophet" or as "his [the Lord's] servant" presented him in a positive light. He is the last in the sequence of prophets in the Northern Kingdom (Ahijah, 1 Kings 11:29–39; 14:1–18; Jehu, 1 Kings 16:7–12; Elijah and Elisha, 1 Kings 17–2 Kings 13; the prophets mentioned in 1 Kings 20:13–22 and 28; Micaiah, 1 Kings 22).

Jonah's hometown is identified in 2 Kings as Gath-hepher, located about fifteen miles west of the Sea of Galilee in the territory of Zebulun (Josh.

---

[3] See pp. 29–30 above.

[4] E.g., Susi is "wild horse," Num. 13:11; Kore is "partridge," 1 Chron. 9:19; Parosh is "flea," Ezra 2:3. See M. Noth, *Die israelitischen Personennamen im Rahmen der gemein-semitischen Namengebung* (Stuttgart: W. Kohlhammer, 1928), 230.

[5] On this theme, see Gese, 122–138.

[6] Josephus comments on Jonah and Jeroboam's campaign, concluding, "So Jeroboam made an expedition against the Syrians, and overran all their country as Jonah had foretold" (*Antiquities* 10); for the complete text, see Appendix 2.1 (pp. 100–101).

19:13). Today the Arab village of Meshed is located where Gath-hepher was, between Nazareth and Kefar Kana (Cana). Meshed, in fact, takes its name from the memory of Jonah. The Arabic *el meshed* means "martyr grave" and a grave of Jonah may be found there.[7]

It is often pointed out that Jonah is never named "prophet" in the book that bears his name. If the book of Jonah was produced sometime during the late exilic or early postexilic period,[8] there would have been no need to identify him further than "Jonah son of Amittai." The hearers in that small community of the faithful would have known who he was, recalling him from the account in 2 Kings as one of the significant figures in the history of the north. He was, after all, called "the prophet" and was identified as a "servant of the Lord" whose word proved to be true. Jonah and Jeroboam, working together, were the two "hands" by which the Lord had delivered Israel. Their combined efforts brought about the longest and the final period of peace and prosperity that the Northern Kingdom would know.

The only further references to Jonah in canonical literature are in Matt. 12:38-41; 16:1-4; and Luke 11:29-32.[9]

[2] The commission given to Jonah follows the typical pattern of a prophetic commissioning: "get up . . . go . . . do" (1 Kings 17:9; cf. Num. 22:20-21). Only Elijah and Jonah among the prophets are sent on missions to foreign lands.

Two things are said about Nineveh as the story opens. It is called "that great city" and is so described again in 3:2; 3:3 (intensified); and 4:11; cf. Judith 1:1. The designation "great" for a city is rare in the Bible. Jerusalem is named "the great city" in the prediction of its destruction in Jer. 22:8, and Gibeon is so named in Josh. 10:2 (NRSV "large"). The opening and closing words of the book of Jonah call to mind the picture of a far-off, sprawling metropolis of ancient times. Nineveh is also described as wicked,

---

[7] See "Gath-Hepher," in *IDB*, E-J, 356; W. F. Albright, "New Israelite and Pre-Israelite Sites: The Spring Trip of 1929," *BASOR* 35 (1929): 8; and Zev Vilnay, *The Guide to Israel* (Jerusalem: Hamakor Press, 1978[20]), 471. Joachim Jeremias discusses three Palestinian traditions about the location of Jonah's grave: the Galilean location goes back at least as far as Jerome's Jonah commentary, written in 395. Another tradition locates the grave near Lydda, southwest of modern Tel Aviv. Still another locates it in the village of Halhul, six kilometers to the north of Hebron. Jeremias concludes his discussion by saying, "As the only prophetic grave in Galilee the Jonah grave must have had very special significance for Galilean Judaism" (*Heiligengräber in Jesu Umwelt*, 28, my translation; see also 88-90; on the modern village of Halhul, see Vilnay, 169). Yet another tradition locates a grave of Jonah in the ruins of Nineveh; see p. 40 below.

[8] See pp. 28-31 above.

[9] See pp. 72-74 below. For references to Jonah in apocryphal/deuterocanonical works, see Appendix 1 (pp. 99-100).

and that "wickedness" has come to the attention of the Lord. Historical and archaeological investigation help one to understand the first attribute of this city; the biblical writers shed light on the second.

Nineveh was located on the east bank of the Tigris River, roughly at the intersection of the Tigris with a line drawn straight east from the northeastern corner of the Mediterranean. The distance from Jonah's home in northern Israel is about five hundred miles by air. The ruins of Nineveh are across the Tigris from the modern city of Mosul in Iraq, two hundred and fifty miles north of Baghdad.

Long one of the chief cities of Mesopotamia, Nineveh was the last capital of the Assyrian empire. Excavations have indicated settlement in the area as early as 6000 B.C.[10] Hammurabi, king of Babylon about 1750 B.C., mentions Nineveh in the prologue to his famous law code as the location of a temple of Inanna.[11] The city continued to grow in importance during the time of the revival of the Assyrian empire, beginning with emperor Tiglath-pileser III (745–727 B.C.). Sennacherib (705–681 B.C.) made it the capital city in 701 B.C. During the days of Esar-haddon (680–669 B.C.) and Assurbanipal (668–627 B.C.) Nineveh was the chief city of the biblical world's most powerful empire. Nineveh fell to the armies of the Medes and Babylonians in 612 B.C. and was left a heap of ruins, never to be rebuilt. Xenophon passed by in 401 B.C. with his retreating Greek army and described what once was Nineveh as "a great stronghold, deserted and lying in ruins."[12] Excavations beginning in the mid-1800s reveal a walled city, somewhat trapezoidal in shape, with a perimeter of about seven and one half miles. Among the significant finds have been some twenty-five thousand tablets of the library of Assurbanipal, including the Babylonian flood story and the Gilgamesh Epic. Two mounds remain at the site, both at the western wall: Kuyunjik, or "the mound of many sheep," and Nebi Yunus, "the prophet Jonah," now the site of a mosque marking the place where the prophet is supposed to be buried.[13]

Nineveh is first mentioned in the Bible in Gen. 10:11–12, where it is said of Nimrod that "he went into Assyria, and built Nineveh"; again it is called "the great city."[14]

---

[10] See "Nineveh," in *Atlas of Ancient Archaeology,* ed. J. Hawkes (New York: McGraw-Hill, 1974), 182; see also *Iraq* 42 (1980): 185–186, and D. J. Wiseman, "Nineveh," *The Illustrated Bible Dictionary,* part 2 (Wheaton, Ill.: Tyndale, 1980), 1089–1092.

[11] *ANET,* 165.

[12] *Anabasis,* books I-VII, trans. C. L. Brownson (London: William Heinemann, 1968), 3.4.10–12.

[13] See S. Lloyd, *The Archaeology of Mesopotamia* (New York: Thames & Hudson, 1984²), "The Late Assyrian Period," 187–201.

[14] So C. Westermann, *Genesis 1–11,* BKAT (Darmstadt: Wissenschaftliche Buchgesellschaft, 1984²), 518. But see the remarks of E. A. Speiser, *Genesis,* AB (Garden City,

Several passages express the attitude of the prophets toward Nineveh and the Assyrians. Speaking a couple of decades before Nineveh's destruction in 612 B.C., Zephaniah announced:

> . . . and he will make Nineveh a desolation,
>   a dry waste like the desert.
> Herds shall lie down in it,
>   every wild animal;
> the desert owl and the screech owl
>   shall lodge on its capitals;
> the owl shall hoot at the window,
>   the raven croak on the threshold;
> for its cedar work will be laid bare.
> Is this the exultant city that dwelt secure,
>   that said to itself, "I am and there is no one else"?
> What a desolation it has become,
>   a lair for wild animals!
> Everyone who passes by it
>   hisses and shakes his fist.
>
>   (Zeph. 2:13-15)

Even more harsh are the words of Nahum, again spoken shortly before Nineveh's fall. The entire book is "an oracle concerning Nineveh" (Nahum 1:1):

> Woe to the bloody city,
>   all full of lies and booty. . . .
> Behold, I am against you,
>   says the LORD of hosts,
>   and will lift up your skirts over your face;
> and I will let nations look on your nakedness
>   and kingdoms on your shame.
> I will throw filth at you
>   and treat you with contempt,
>   and make you a gazingstock. . . .
> Wasted is Nineveh; who will bemoan her?
>   (Nahum 3:1-7, RSV)

No one will grieve when Nineveh falls, says the prophet. The book ends: "All who hear the news of you clap their hands over you. For upon whom has not come your unceasing evil?" (Nahum 3:19).

Both of these prophets give reasons for Nineveh's destruction. Zephaniah hints at pride (Zeph. 2:15). According to Nahum, Nineveh has plotted

---

N.Y.: Doubleday & Co., 1964), 68, who applies the expression to Calah. See also 2 Kings 19:36.

against the Lord (Nahum 1:9), is worthless (1:14) and a ferocious lion (2:11–12). The city is filled with lies and plunder (3:1) and has acted like a faithless whore toward other nations (3:4). All have experienced her evil (3:19).

The command to Jonah, "Get up, go to Nineveh," should be heard against the background of this picture of Nineveh painted by these prophets.

[3] Following the usual biblical pattern (Num. 22:20–21; 1 Kings 17:8–10), we would expect the narrative to continue, "So Jonah got up and went to Nineveh." But Jonah has his own itinerary. Told to set out for Nineveh to the northeast of his hometown of Gath-hepher, he heads off in the opposite direction, toward the port of Joppa to the southwest. Here is another reminiscence of Elijah: that prophet once ran away to Beer-sheba because of a threat from Jezebel (1 Kings 19:2–3). Uriah also ran away, to Egypt, because King Jehoiakim did not like what he had said (Jer. 26:20–23). Jonah, however, is the only one of the prophets to run away even before delivering his message.

Why does Jonah not want to carry out an assignment in Nineveh? His words in 4:2 provide a clue: Nineveh might repent, the Lord might forgive them, and Jonah does not want that. The words of Nahum and Zephaniah cited above help to explain this Israelite's hostility toward the Assyrians.

Josephus suggests that fear motivated Jonah to run away: "But he went not, out of fear; nay, he ran away from God to the city of Joppa."[15]

Another suggestion is given in the first-century A.D. *Lives of the Prophets.* If Jonah prophesied against Nineveh and Nineveh was not destroyed, then Jonah would look like a false prophet. In the following quotation he appears to think of himself that way:

> And when he had been cast forth by the sea monster and had gone away to Nineveh and had returned, he did not remain in his district, but taking his mother along he sojourned in Sour, a territory (inhabited by) foreign nations; for he said, "So shall I remove my reproach, for I spoke falsely in prophesying against the great city of Nineveh."[16]

The ninth-century A.D. *Pirke de Rabbi Eliezer* suggests that Jonah did not want to go to Nineveh, because he suspected that Nineveh might repent and God would forgive. Then the Lord would be angry with Israel for

---

[15] Josephus, *Antiquities of the Jews,* in *Complete Works,* trans. W. Whiston (Grand Rapids: Kregel Publications, 1960), 207. For the complete text, see Appendix.

[16] *OTP,* 2:392. The account subsequently identifies Jonah and his mother as the couple visited by Elijah; when the son (Jonah) died, Elijah raised him up "to show him that it is not possible to run away from God." See Appendix for the longer quote from *Lives of the Prophets.*

being so slow to repent and Jonah, who had announced Nineveh's destruction, would be seen as a lying prophet.[17]

The precise location of Tarshish is uncertain. Josephus identified it with Tarsus in Asia Minor.[18] The Targum translated simply, "to go with them to sea."[19] A survey of biblical references indicates that it is a place far removed from Israel; it is listed along with the nations and "the coastlands afar off, that have not heard my fame or seen my glory" (Isa. 66:19). Psalm 72 expresses the wish that royalty from Sheba and Seba (in southern Arabia) and from Tarshish and the islands will pay homage (Ps. 72:10). Solomon had a fleet of ships at sea that brought exotic cargoes from Tarshish to Jerusalem once every three years (1 Kings 10:22). From that time on, the Bible makes frequent reference to "Tarshish ships" (NRSV "ships of the Tarshish type," 1 Kings 22:48) to designate vessels capable of long voyages. These ships were noted for their size and are listed among those things which are "proud and lofty" (Isa. 2:16; cf. also 2 Chron. 20:36–37; Isa. 23:1, 14; 60:9; Ezek. 27:25; Ps. 48:7 [8]). The most common suggestion for locating Tarshish connects it with Tartessos, on the southwestern Spanish coast.[20] In any case, the function of Tarshish in the story is clear: Jonah is planning to set out toward the farthest point in the opposite direction from Nineveh.

The expression "away from the presence of the LORD" is doubled, to emphasize the point (1:10 picks it up again, recalling these same events). Of course the hearers of the story knew that such a running away from the Lord was impossible, recalling words like Ps. 139:7 "Where can I go from your spirit? Or where can I flee from your presence?" Only Cain, the murderer, is described in the Bible as making a similar attempt to run "away from the presence of the LORD" (Gen. 4:16).

Four times the story reports that Jonah "goes down." Here, he goes down to Joppa and then down to the ship. He will go down into the hold (1:5) and finally to the bottom of the mountains in the sea (2:6). The narrative is indicating how Jonah is totally separating himself from God, both horizontally (toward Tarshish) and vertically (toward the bottom of the sea).[21]

The location of Joppa has remained the same; it is mentioned as a port

---

[17] See Appendix, pp. 104–105.

[18] *Antiquities,* 10; see Appendix 2.1 (pp. 100–101).

[19] Cathcart and Gordon, 105.

[20] So, e.g., M. Noth, *Könige,* vol. I, BKAT, IX/1 (Neukirchen-Vluyn: Neukirchener Verlag, 1968), 232; and Wolff, *Obadiah and Jonah,* 100–101. Sasson (p. 79) surveys the discussion and concludes, "*Tarsis* seems always to lie just beyond the geographic knowledge of those who try to pinpoint its location."

[21] See Magonet, "Jonah, Book of," *ABD.*

in 2 Chron. 2:16; Ezra 3:7; cf. 1 Macc. 10:76. Joppa appears in the New Testament (Acts 9:36–43) and is today Yafo, near Tel Aviv.[22]

Since the Hebrew text says literally that Jonah "paid its fare," some traditional Jewish commentators have suggested that the prophet picked up the tab for all aboard.[23]

In the *Zohar,* Rabbi Abba understands Jonah's descent into the ship as an allegory of the soul's descent into the world:

> In the story of Jonah we have a representation of the whole of a man's career in this world. Jonah descending into the ship is symbolic of man's soul that descends into this world to enter into his body. . . . Man, then, is in this world as in a ship that is traversing the great ocean and is like to be broken."[24]

If there is some uncertainty about the location of Tarshish, there is no lack of clarity about what Jonah is trying to do. "Tarshish" as the direction of disobedience rings three times, for emphasis. The doubled "from the presence of the LORD" puts a theological perspective on Jonah's actions.

A story "narrates a series of events from a point of tension to the resolution of that tension."[25] The tension driving this story has now been set. What will happen to a prophet who disobeys the Lord's command and tries to run away? And what will happen to Nineveh, that great — but wicked — city? Scenes II (1:4–16) and III (1:17–2:10 [2:1–11]) deal with the first of these questions. Scenes IV (3:1–3a) and V (3:3b–10) deal with the second, and scenes VI (4:1–3) and VII (4:4–10) are concerned with both.

That which strikes one about this first scene in the story of Jonah is the strong theological interest it exhibits. The narrator speaks of the Lord at the beginning, in the middle, and at the end of the scene. This explicit theological concern continues to run through the entire narrative. The first, fourth, and final scenes are set in motion with words of the Lord (1:1; 3:1; 4:4); the second and third scenes are introduced with acts of the Lord (1:4; 1:17); and the sixth scene is introduced with Jonah's reaction to God's action (4:1). The first two scenes end with the Lord as the object of the action (1:3, 16), the third and fifth scenes conclude with the Lord/God as the subject of the action (2:10; 3:10), and the entire book concludes with a word from the Lord (4:10–11).

---

[22] Joppa was noted as a place where sagas about sea monsters were told; see Steffen, *Mysterium,* part 4.

[23] Wünsche, 40.

[24] *Zohar,* 4:173; see Appendix 3.2 (pp. 108–109).

[25] Westermann; see p. 24 above.

Excursus: The Names for God in Jonah

In the book of Jonah, the name Lord (Heb., *Yahweh*) is mentioned 22 times, God (Heb., *Elohim* or *El*, once) 13 times, and the combination Lord God four times for a total of 39 references to the deity in 48 verses. This explicitly theological language, already evident here in scene I, sets the book of Jonah apart, for example, from other narrative books such as Ruth, in which the narrator (not the characters in the story) mentions the Lord only twice (Ruth 1:8; 4:13; the narrator in Jonah uses Lord or God a total of 26 times), and Esther, in which God is not mentioned at all. The question is, Is there a pattern in the use of the divine names, or is the usage random?[26]

1. The names for God are distributed as follows:

```
Yahweh:  1:1, 3, 3, 4, 10, 14, 14, 14, 16, 16      = 10
         [2:1, 3, 8, 10, 11] = 1:17; 2:2, 7, 9, 10  =  5
         3:1, 3                                      =  2
         4:2, 2, 3, 4, 10                            =  5
                                                 22 times
Elohim:  1:5, 6, 6
         3:3, 5, 8, 9, 10, 10
         4:2 (El), 7, 8, 9                         13 times
Yahweh Elohim: 1:9; 2:[2, 7]1, 6; 4:6               4 times
```

2. Jonah 1:1–16 suggests a pattern in name usage. Yahweh is used to refer to the God of the Hebrews, and Elohim is used in connection with the gods of the non-Israelite sailors and their captain, in 1:5 and 6 (twice). The sailors hear about Yahweh from Jonah (1:9), and in 1:14–15 they are addressing and worshiping Yahweh. In his climactic statement in 1:9, Jonah identifies Yahweh as the God of heaven and the maker of the sea and the dry land.

The same pattern may be observed in 1:17–2:10 [2:1–11]. Yahweh is used by the narrator or by Jonah in his prayer. The compound form "Yahweh Elohim" is used by the narrator (2:1 [2]) and by Jonah (2:6 [7]).

In Jonah 3, Yahweh occurs only twice, in both instances used by the narrator as part of a fixed formula. The focus of the two scenes in this chapter is the non-Israelite city of Nineveh. The king of Nineveh, who has not learned to know Yahweh, speaks of Elohim or God (3:8, 9). The narrator uses Elohim in a superlative construction (3:3; see the commentary) and then in describing the faith of the Ninevites (3:10 twice) who have not

---

[26] Among recent commentators, Sasson (p. 18) and Rudolph (p. 367) see no pattern; Stuart (p. 438) considers the usage "not easily explained."

yet learned to konw God as Yahweh. In sum, in these first three chapters, "Yahweh" is used to refer to God as the Hebrews have learned to know God, and "Elohim" is used to refer to the deity the non-Israelites know.

The name usage in 4:1–5 can be explained according to the same principle. Jonah is addressing Yahweh, the name revealed to the Hebrews. The use of "El," God, in 4:2 may be explained by the fact that this is a traditional creedal formulation (cf. Ex. 34:6; Ps. 86:15; Neh. 9:31).

The narrator's use of Elohim in 4:7, 8, and 9, and of Yahweh again in 4:10, presents a more difficult problem.

Jonathan Magonet has suggested an explanation that is both simple and compelling. When the narrator is speaking of divine punishing action, the narrator uses the more general term, Elohim or God. Thus God (Elohim) punished Jonah by appointing a worm to attack the plant (4:7), then God (Elohim) appointed a hot wind to attack Jonah (4:8), and it is God (Elohim), who has been disciplining the prophet, who addresses Jonah in 4:9. In 4:10, however, where the emphasis is on divine grace, mercy, and care, the more personal designation Yahweh again appears. The compound form Yahweh Elohim (Lord God) in 4:6 makes the transition.[27]

Given the intense theological interest in the book of Jonah, what does this opening scene say about God?

It is clear that for the author of Jonah, the Lord is more than a local or tribal god. The worldwide, ecumenical focus of the book is evident from the first sentence. The story begins with a declaration of the Lord's concern for far-off Nineveh, indicating that the Lord is a God who cares about the great cities and nations of the earth. This broad theological horizon is, of course, not new with the book of Jonah. Considering Jonah in the context of the Book of the Twelve, we observe that Amos has indicated the Lord's concern for the nations of the world (Amos 1–2) and Obadiah delivered a prophetic oracle about Edom. This same international horizon is also evident in the book of Micah (1:2; 4:1–5; 5:4; 7:16–17) and with Nahum, where the spotlight is once again on Nineveh.

The artist Michelangelo understood something of the worldwide orientation of the book of Jonah. His work in the Sistine Chapel in Rome was done during the Renaissance, during the age of the world explorations of Columbus and Magellan. The artist's depiction of Jonah is located front and center in the chapel, just above the famous portrayal of the Last Judgment. The prophet looks toward heaven, his left arm thrown across his twisted body. He appears to be recoiling from something he sees. In the background lurks the massive head of the great fish. On the ceiling of the

---

[27] See Magonet, *Form,* 33–38; cf. also Gese, 267.

chapel is a series of scenes from the creation to Noah. Along the sides of the chapel ceiling are the prophets Jeremiah, Ezekiel, Joel, Zechariah, Isaiah, and Daniel. Alternating with these biblical prophets are five sibyls, priestesses from the classical world, searching through their sacred books. In a somewhat remarkable affirmation of these non-Hebrew traditions, the chapel paintings seem to be saying: God's revelation came through the Hebrew prophets, but through these Gentiles too! Jonah, as the only one of the major or minor prophets to address a nation other than Israel, seems quite at home in this ecumenical context.[28]

What does the opening scene say about God and Jonah? This remains a question. The Lord speaks to Jonah in the manner in which the Lord has spoken to the other prophets of Israel and Judah. But when a prophet runs away from his assignment, then what? Twice the narrator labels this action as attempting to escape from the "presence of the LORD." How will the Lord, who is concerned about the great nations of the earth, react to the rebellion of one individual? What will happen to one who tries to escape one's calling by running away from the Lord? The answers to these questions await the telling of the story.

The Storm
1:4–16

Scene I closed with Jonah running away from the Lord. Scene II (1:4–16) opens by describing the Lord's reaction to Jonah's flight, as the Lord "hurls" a storm on the sea. The tension that animates the scene is introduced immediately: Will the ship break up and all aboard perish (1:4)?

The scene opens with the sending of a storm and closes with the storm stopping. It is framed with the report that the Lord hurled a wind and the sailors hurled Jonah. The entire scene is built according to a concentric or chiastic pattern:

> A The Lord hurls storm (1:4)
>> B Sailors pray, act (1:5ab)
>>> C Jonah acts (lies down, sleeps; 1:5c)
>>>> D Captain, sailors question Jonah (1:6–8)
>>>>> E Jonah speaks (1:9)
>>>> D' Sailors question Jonah (1:10–11)
>>> C' Jonah speaks ("hurl me"; 1:12)
>> B' Sailors act, pray (1:13–14)
> A' Sailors hurl Jonah, storm ends (1:15)
> Conclusion (1:16)

---

[28] See *Bible Review* 6 (August 1990): 23–25 for discussion and illustrations.

Jonah's words in 1:9, a confession of faith, have been carefully placed at the midpoint of this concentric structure. There are 94 words in the Hebrew text from the scene's beginning in 1:4 to the beginning of the speech in 1:9 ("I am a Hebrew") and 94 words in 1:10-15. Verse 16 stands outside the pattern as a conclusion. Both the concentric structure and the exact balance of number of words serve to place the focus for this section on the confession in 1:9.[29]

4 But the LORD hurled a great wind upon the sea, and there was a great storm on the sea, so that the ship threatened to break up.

[4] Scene I ended with the statement that Jonah was running away from the Lord. Scene II begins with an emphasis on the Lord's reaction, by placing the Hebrew subject before the verb, "But the LORD . . . ."[30]

Here are two examples of the narrator's fondness for repeating words throughout the story.[31] Just as Saul "hurled" his spear at David (1 Sam. 18:11) or at Jonathan (1 Sam. 20:33), so the Lord took "a great wind" from his heavenly arsenal and "hurled" it upon the sea. As the story continues, the author plays upon the word: the sailors "hurl" the cargo into the sea (1:5), Jonah suggests that the sailors "hurl" him into the sea (1:12), and they do so (1:15). "Great" is one of the narrator's favorite words, occurring fourteen times.[32] "Great storm" occurs only here and in Jer. 25:32 (NRSV "tempest").

The verb "threatened" (lit., "had a mind to") is ordinarily used to indicate the thinking or planning activity of a human being (Mal. 3:16, "thought") or of God (Gen. 50:20, "intended"). Only here does it have an inanimate subject, perhaps reflecting the personifying style of storytelling ("the ship

---

[29] For another example of numerical balance in Jonah, see Jonah 4. There are other biblical examples of the central assertion of a piece being placed in the numerical middle. The words "for you are with me" in Psalm 23, e.g., are in the numerical middle, with twenty-six words before and after in the Hebrew text. This section has been analyzed in a variety of more or less sophisticated manners. Weimar, e.g., sees a frame in 1:4 + 5a and 15-16, A and A' in 1:5b + 6 and 14, B and B' in 1:7 and 12-13, C and C' in 1:8 and 11, and the middle in 1:9-10 ("Literarische Kritik und Literarkritik"). In any case, the structure is clearly concentric; I prefer my analysis because of the "hurl" inclusio and also the balance in the number of words, though admitting that v. 16 stands outside the structure.

[30] The subject in emphatic position before the verb is found in *narrative contexts* in Jonah: 1:4b ("and the ship"); 1:5 ("and Jonah"); 1:14 ("for you are the LORD"); 3:3b ("now as for Nineveh"); 3:7b ("no human being"); 4:10 ("you are concerned about"); and 4:11 ("and I, should I not"); and in *poetic contexts:* 2:3 [4] ("and the flood . . . all your breakers and your waves"); 2:4 [5] ("and as for me"); 2:5 [6] ("the deep"); 2:10 [11] ("and I"). For syntactical observations, see R. J. Williams, *Hebrew Syntax* (Toronto: University of Toronto Press, 1967), 573.

[31] See p. 27 above.

[32] See p. 27 above.

thought it would break up").[33] This is in fact one of the few examples of personification in Jonah.[34] The Hebrew gives "the ship" some extra emphasis here, again placing the subject before the verb. The Masoretic punctuation also emphasizes the word, marking a pause after "ship"; thus a literal reading, "and as for the ship — it had a mind to break up."

5ab Then the sailors were afraid, and each cried to his god; and they hurled the cargo that was in the ship into the sea, to make it lighter for them. 5c And Jonah? He had gone down into the hold of the vessel and had lain down and fallen asleep.

[5ab] The word translated "sailors" occurs only here and in Ezekiel 27, where "the good ship Tyre" is described (Ezek. 27:9, 27, 29). That text gives some idea of the sort of vessel that was sailing the Mediterranean in the sixth century B.C., with fir planks, a mast of cedar, pine deck (27:5–6), and powered both by oars made of oak (27:6) and by linen sails (27:7). The words "were afraid" and "cried to" are used in parallel only here and in Ex. 14:10; this is one of many reminiscences of Exodus 14 in the Jonah story.[35]

Confronted with this storm at sea, the sailors do two things. First, they pray: "each cried to his god." Nothing is said about their manner of praying, and no judgments are made about the efficacy of these prayers. The narrator portrays these sailors in the most favorable light. "Most sailors are pious," says the Talmud.[36] "He that will learn to pray, let him go to sea," goes the proverb. A cry for divine help would be quite appropriate in such a situation, as is apparent from Ps. 107:23–32; the psalm uses this same language for people in distress at sea: "Then they cried to the LORD" (v. 28). According to Jewish tradition, representatives of the seventy nations on earth were on board the ship.[37] Second, just as the Lord had "hurled" the storm on the sea in the first place, "they hurled the cargo that was in the ship into the sea." A ship on the Mediterranean in the sixth century B.C. might carry such cargo as precious metals, horses and mules, ivory, and various other products (Ezek. 27:12–25). The word translated in Jonah

---

[33] Cf. the personification in the fable in Judg. 9:8–15.

[34] See p. 27 above.

[35] See Vanoni (p. 144), who also points to Jonah 1:9, 13 "sea . . . dry land" and Ex. 14:16, 22, 29; Jonah 1:16 "feared . . . the Lord" and Ex. 14:31; Jonah 3:5 "and they believed in God" only here and Ex. 14:31; Jonah 4:2 "was this not what I said" only here and Ex. 14:12.

[36] The full quotation: "R. Judah said in his name: Most ass-drivers are wicked, while most camel drivers are worthy men; and most sailors are pious" (*Kiddushim* 82a, *The Babylonian Talmud: Seder Nashim* [London: Soncino Press, 1936], 423).

[37] "Rabbi Chanina said: (Men) of the seventy languages were there on the ship, and each one had his god in his hand" (from *Pirke de Rabbi Eliezer;* see Appendix, p. 105).

as "cargo" appears in Ezek. 27:13 as "vessels" ("of bronze"). For similar procedures during another Mediterranean storm, see Acts 27:18-19, 38.[38]

[5c] The Lord has hurled the storm and the sailors have been praying and hurling the cargo into the sea. What has Jonah been doing all this time? Once again the narrator emphasizes the subject of a sentence by pulling it around in front of the verb; the translation tries to catch that emphasis with, "And Jonah?" This is the third "going down" of Jonah. Just as the ship heading west moved him across the horizon in the direction of rebellion, so his descent continues, moving him in a vertical direction farther and farther away from God.[39]

Jonah "had lain down and fallen asleep." The same vocabulary is used for an anesthetized-like sleep (Gen. 2:21), for the sleep of the slothful (Prov. 10:5; 19:15) or of the visionary (Dan. 8:18, "trance"; Job 4:13, "deep sleep"). It describes Sisera as in such deep slumber that he didn't hear Jael coming near to deliver his death blow (Judg. 4:21). In the same way, Jonah was sleeping so soundly that he was not aware of the storm, nor of the activity on board the ship, nor of the approach of the captain.

6 So the captain came to him and said, "What are you doing, sleeping?! Get up, call on your god! Perhaps the god will give us a thought and we will not die!"   7 And they said to one another, "Come, let us cast lots so that we may know on whose account this evil has come upon us." So they cast lots, and the lot fell on Jonah.   8 And they said to him, "Tell us now, because of whom has this evil come upon us?[40] What is your occupation? And where do you come from? What is your country? And of what people are you?"

[6] Now a new character comes onto the scene. This is "the captain," literally the "chief of the ropers."[41] The captain puts an angry and accusing question to Jonah: "What are you doing, sleeping?" or, more literally, "What's with you, sleeper?"[42] This same formulation in an accusing question, always in the mouth of a superior to an inferior party, may be observed in Gen. 20:9; Isa. 3:15; 22:1; Ezek. 18:2; and cf. John 2:4. See also the Lord's question to Elijah in 1 Kings 19:9.

The captain's order to "Get up, call on your god!" is the second time Jonah has been told to get up and call/cry out; the vocabulary is the same

---

[38] For some interesting information about ships and ancient lore about storms, see Sasson, 81–82 and 90–92.

[39] See the comments on 1:3.

[40] "Because . . . upon us" is missing in Greek manuscripts Sinaiticus, Vaticanus, and Venetus. Since this may be explained as haplography due to homoioteleuton, *lānû,* the MT should be retained. See Ziegler, *Duodecim prophetae,* 245 (see p. 33 n. 36 above).

[41] Cf. Ezek. 27:27, 29, where the same Hebrew word is translated as "mariners."

[42] Jonah is often drawn into the action with a question; see p. 25 n. 9.

as the Lord's initial commission to Jonah, there translated "preach" (1:2). The captain, who is not an Israelite, is nonetheless a man of piety. When he finds Jonah sleeping, his first action is not to punish him, nor even to ask him to help throw cargo overboard, but to ask him to pray. His is a positive and ecumenical piety. He assumes that Jonah worships some god and also that calling upon that god will help in this acute situation.

The "perhaps" marks another admirable feature of the captain's piety. He does not presume to predict the actions of Jonah's god. Like another non-Israelite, the king of Nineveh, he does not pretend to control God (3:9). "Perhaps" the god of Jonah will help; compare the attitude of Balaam in Num. 23:3 or of the priests who speak to the Philistines in 1 Sam. 6:5: God cannot be controlled. "Behind this 'perhaps,'" suggests Wilhelm Rudolph, "is the experience of unanswered prayer."[43] The verb translated "give us a thought" appears only here in the Old Testament; the Aramaic cognate occurs in Dan. 6:3 [4]; related nouns are in Job 12:5; Ps. 146:4; and Sir. 3:24. The Targum paraphrases here: "perhaps there will be mercy from the Lord upon us."[44]

The Jonah story deals with matters of life and death. Three times that concern is expressed. Here it is the captain who says, "so that we do not die." A short time later the sailors pray to the Lord that they might not die (1:14), and in 3:9 it is the king of Nineveh who hopes that God might change his mind "and we will not die." In each case it is these non-Israelites who are aware that they are in a life-or-death situation. But Jonah, so far as we are told, does not pray.

[7] The sailors make two theological assumptions with their suggestion to "cast lots": (1) the storm is a divine punishment for the misdeed of someone on board the ship;[45] and (2) God communicates through the casting of lots. The Hebrew word *gôrāl,* translated "lot," is related to the Arabic word for stone: *ğarila* (be stony) or *ğarwal* (small stone).[46] The process involved putting stones into the lap of one's garment or into a container and shaking it until a stone came out. According to Prov. 16:33, decisions made by casting lots are from the Lord. In a community that

---

[43] Rudolph, 341 (my translation).

[44] Cathcart and Gordon, 106.

[45] Josephus remarks, "But as the waves grew greater, and the sea became more violent by the winds, they suspected, as is usual in such cases, that some one of the persons that sailed with them was the occasion of this storm, and agreed to discover by lot which of them it was" (*Antiquities* 10; see Appendix). Bickermann observes: "The ship that transports an enemy of the gods is always in danger. In the fifth century, in Athens, Antiphon, a contemporary of Socrates, sought to demonstrate before a court that his client, accused of murder, was innocent because the ship in which he voyaged arrived safely in port" ("Les deux erreurs du prophète Jonas," 37, my translation).

[46] KB[3], 195. See Lindblom, "Lot-casting in the Old Testament," *VT* 12 (1962): 164ff.

accepts the validity of the procedure, "casting the lot puts an end to disputes" (Prov. 18:18).

The procedure could be used in connection with choices affecting the future. Lots were used for choosing a king (1 Sam. 10:20–21), or the leaders of an attack (Judg. 20:9), or a favorable day for an action (Esth. 3:7), or a goat to be sacrificed for Yom Kippur (Lev. 16:8), or the residents for the city of Jerusalem (Neh. 11:1). Lots were often used for dividing up things and people, such as land[47] (Josh. 18:6), clothing of one about to die (Ps. 22:18; Matt. 27:35; Mark 15:24; Luke 23:34), duties at the temple (1 Chron. 25:8; 26:14; Neh. 10:34), or prisoners taken after a victory (Joel 3:3; Obad. 11; Nahum 3:10; cf. also Sir. 37:8). The New Testament indicates an addition to the process: when a replacement was needed for Judas, the procedure involved not only the casting of lots but also the prayer of the congregation (Acts 1:15–26). The New Testament expression is the same as the Greek account of Jonah:

> *kai epesen ho klēros epi Maththian* (Acts 1:26)
> *kai epesen ho klēros epi Iōnan* (Jonah 1:7, LXX)

Lot casting also functioned in connection with the past. A party guilty of committing an offense might be detected by lot (Josh. 7:14–26). Sometimes the decision of the lot could be overridden by the people (1 Sam. 14:36–46), indicating that the method was not always a foolproof indication of the mind of the Lord! It is this second sort of lot casting which takes place in Jonah. The exact procedure is not described; it would have been familiar to the first hearers of the story.

The technique works. The lots are cast, and the stone indicating the guilty party is the one belonging to Jonah.[48]

[8] Again the sailors are described in a favorable manner. In the midst of this storm at sea they are calm, reasonable, and fair men. Even though the lot has fallen upon Jonah, they do not immediately assume his guilt, nor are they immediately ready to throw him overboard. They give him a chance to say something about himself in his own defense. They do assume that the storm is a punishment because of the actions of some person.

The sailors fire a barrage of four questions at Jonah: "What is your business?" Psalm 107:23 uses the same word to refer to the work of those involved in the business of shipping; Prov. 18:9 describes those who are slack in their work (business) and Prov. 22:29 describes those who are

---

[47] Cf. English "lot" for portion of land.

[48] In the Arabic *Tales of the Prophets of al-Kisa'i*, names are written on lead balls which are thrown into the sea; see Appendix, p. 116.

skillful at it. "And where do you come from?" See Judg. 17:9; 19:17 for the same formulation. "What is your country? And of what people are you?" Second Samuel 15:2 uses the same words when Absalom asks those coming to Jerusalem, "From what city are you?"

9 And he said to them, "I am a Hebrew, and I worship the LORD, the God of heaven, who made the sea and the dry land."

[9] For the first time in the story, Jonah speaks. The author puts the spotlight on Jonah's speech by placing it at the exact midpoint of scene II.[49] His words "A Hebrew am I" (the literal word order) are unique in the Bible and come as an answer to the question, "And of what people are you?" This ethnological sense of "Hebrew," where it is synonymous with "one of the people of Israel," carries over into the New Testament in Paul's words in Phil. 3:5. In earlier texts in the Old Testament, "Hebrew" is used by foreigners when referring to Israelites (Egyptians: Gen. 39:14, 17; 41:12; Philistines: 1 Sam. 4:6, 9; 13:19) or when the text marks a contrast between Israelites and other people (Gen. 43:32). First Samuel 14:21 indicates that the class "Hebrews" includes more than Israelites.[50] The expression "the LORD, the God of heaven" also occurs in Gen. 24:7 (24:3, "heaven and earth," Abraham speaks); 2 Chron. 36:23 and Ezra 1:2 (Cyrus speaks); and Neh. 1:5 (Nehemiah prays), thus always in direct address.[51] "I worship" is literally, "I fear." The sense is to honor and have regard for, as children ought to relate to parents (Lev. 19:3, "revere") or as the Israelites regarded Joshua (Josh. 4:14, "stand in awe"). This is the proper attitude toward the Lord (see Ex. 14:31; Josh. 24:14, NRSV "revere") and is often best translated "worship" (2 Kings 17:25, 28, 32, 33, 34, 41); see also Pss. 15:4; 22:23; 112:1; for the cognate noun, Prov. 1:7; 2:5; etc.

Jonah speaks of the God "who made the sea and the dry land." God's creating action may be called "making": Gen. 1:7, 16, 25; Neh. 9:6; Job 9:9; Prov. 8:26; esp. Ps. 95:5, "The sea is his, for he made it, and the dry land, which his hands have formed." God created both sea and dry land (Gen. 1:9–10). The totality is indicated by naming the extremes

---

[49] See pp. 47–48 above.

[50] See von Rad in *TDNT*, 3:359. Though the issue is debated, "Hebrew" may have originally had a sociological meaning. It is apparently related to the term *Hapiru*, which denoted "a class of people without citizenship, who lived on the fringes of the existing social structure, without roots or fixed place in it" (J. Bright, *A History of Israel* [Philadelphia: Westminster Press, 1981³], 95); but see further Sasson, 116–117. The Septuagint translates *doulos kyriou*, "I am a servant of the Lord"; the Hebrew *'ibrî* (a Hebrew) was misread as *'ebed y[hwh]* (servant of Yahweh; cf. 2 Kings 14:25).

[51] "The God of heaven" is especially frequent in later literature of the Old Testament: in Hebrew in Neh. 1:4; 2:4; cf. also Ps. 136:26, and in its Aramaic equivalent in Ezra (5:11, 12; 6:9, 10; 7:12, 21, 23 twice) and Daniel (2:18, 19, 37, 44).

(merismus).[52] The mere mention of "dry land" must have sounded good to Jonah and those around him! The word comes up two more times in Jonah: the men try to row the ship back to the land (1:13) and Jonah is spit up upon it (2:10[11]). Wolff comments: "This is the first indication, even though in highly restrained terms, that there is some connection or other between Jonah and the storm."[53]

What Jonah says throughout the narrative indicates that he has a mastery of the essentials of his faith. In addition to this confession, we hear his prayer in 2:2-9 which is formulated in the typical language of Hebrew prayer, his brief proclamation in Nineveh in 3:4, and his recital of a traditional statement about God in 4:2. Whatever Jonah's problems may be, knowledge about the faith is not one of them! He can recite orthodox confessions and he knows how to pray.

To this point Jonah has answered only the last of the questions put to him, saying nothing about his occupation, home, or country. While the sailors did not ask about his religious preference, he has volunteered that information in a confession of faith in the Lord who made the sea and the dry land.

10 Then the men were very much afraid,[54] and they said to him, "What is this that you have done?" For the men knew that he was running away from the presence of the LORD, because he had told them. 11 Then they said to him, "What shall we do to you, to make the sea calm around us?" For the sea kept on[55] storming.

[10] Verse 5 indicated that the sailors were afraid because of the storm. Now the description of their fear is intensified; they literally "fear a great fear." The second half of the verse explains their fear: Jonah had told them he was running away from the Lord (cf. 1:3). Now everything has changed for the sailors. Something uncanny is going on! They have a hunch that this terrifying storm has theological dimensions. It must be some sort of divine punishment. The crew are appalled at what they have just heard from this passenger and they ask, "What is this that you have done?" The formulation is the same as the question put to the woman in the garden (Gen. 3:13). These "What" (Heb., *mah*) questions ring through the story: "What are you doing, sleeping?!" (1:6); "What is your occupation?" "What is your country?" (1:8); and immediately following:

---

[52] See p. 27 above for more examples.

[53] Wolff, *Obadiah and Jonah*, 115.

[54] The cognate accusative expresses emphasis; see GKC, 117q. Cognate accusatives indicating emphasis in Jonah occur in pairs: 1:10 and 16a indicate intensification of the same action, while 4:1 and 6 indicate contrast. Cf. also 1:16b; 3:2.

[55] The participle *hôlēk* here expresses continuing action; GKC, 113u.

[11] "What shall we do to you . . . ?" The captain had put the first question to Jonah (1:6). Now with this seventh question from the sailors, the interrogation is complete. Jonah himself has made it clear that there is some mysterious connection between himself and the storm. The "growing phrases" of vs. 4, 11, and 13 indicate the worsening of the situation. Similar vocabulary again points to Psalm 107 as a commentary on this storm scene: "calm down," translated "quiet" in Ps. 107:30; storming, cf. "stormy" of Ps. 107:25 and "storm" in 107:29.

12 Then he said to them, "Pick me up and hurl me into the sea, and the sea will calm down around you. For I know that this great storm has come upon you because of me."

[12] Once again Jonah speaks only in response to the sailors' questions. The answer is very direct: "Pick me up and hurl me into the sea." The sailors have "hurled" (1:5) the cargo overboard, and now, using the same verb, Jonah himself asks to be treated like just so much more excess baggage. This will not be the last time Jonah expresses a death wish (4:3, 8).

13 And the men rowed hard to try to return to the dry land, but they could not do it, because the sea kept on storming against them. 14 Then they cried out to the LORD, and they said, "O please, LORD, do not let us die because of this man's life, and do not hold us guilty of shedding innocent blood. For you are the LORD! And whatever you wish, you do."⁵⁶

[13] The literal sense of the verb "rowed" is "dig," as one might dig through a wall (Ezek. 8:8; 12:5). Here the crew dig their oars into the water. The worsening of the storm is indicated by the escalating intensity of each description:

> "and there was a great storm on the sea" (1:4)
> "for the sea kept on storming" (1:11)
> "for the sea kept on storming against them" (1:13)⁵⁷

[14] The captain had asked Jonah to call upon his god, hoping that Jonah's god would act and that all would not perish (1:6), but Jonah has not done so. Once again the sailors, the non-Israelite outsiders, are put in the more favorable light. It is they who "cried out to the LORD." The narrator is again developing variations on a thematic Hebrew word: The Lord had told Jonah to preach/call out against Nineveh (1:2); Jonah elected not to. The captain asked Jonah to call upon his god in prayer (1:6); again,

---

⁵⁶ The parallel expressions in Ps. 115:3 and esp. Ps. 135:6 suggest this translation. This sounds more like a general statement (as in Ps. 135:6) than a reference to a specific act of God; cf. Sasson (pp. 135–136).

⁵⁷ Another example of the "growing phrase"; cf. 1:5, 10, 16, and Magonet, *Form,* 31–33.

Jonah does not do so. If Jonah, the insider who has experienced a direct word from the Lord, will not cry out to his God, then the sailors, the outsiders, will, and they do.

The prayer of the sailors is phrased in the most urgent language of entreaty, using the particles *'ānnāh* and *nā'*, "O please." This same language of entreaty, translated in a variety of ways, appears in other life-and-death situations: Joseph's brothers, fearing for their lives (Gen. 50:17, "I beg you"), Hezekiah's desperate prayer on his sickbed (2 Kings 20:3 = Isa. 38:3, "I implore you"), and the doubled petition in Ps. 118:25, "we beseech you." For *'ānnāh* alone, see Ex. 32:31 ("Alas") and Ps. 116:4 ("I pray").

To be guilty of "innocent blood" means to kill an innocent person (cf. Deut. 27:25; Jer. 26:15). On the national scale, this had been the crime of Egypt and Edom (Joel 3:19) and of kings in Judah like Jehoiakim (Jer. 22:17) and Manasseh (2 Kings 21:16; 24:4) as well as the people of Israel as a whole (Isa. 59:7; Jer. 2:34; 19:4). This is what the sailors were worried about in regard to Jonah. Israel's legal (Deut. 19:10, 13; 27:25) as well as wisdom traditions (Prov. 6:17) warned against the killing of an innocent person, and Deut. 21:1–9 offers a procedure for purging the guilt of a community when a murder by an unknown person has taken an innocent life. Once again, these sailors are portrayed in a most favorable manner. The Israelites have had a history of taking innocent blood (Jer. 2:34; 19:4; Isa. 59:7; etc.); these non-Israelites are most concerned not to do so. The sailors leave the door open for the maker of the sea and the dry land (1:9) to perform a rescue with their words, "For you are the LORD![58] And whatever you wish, you do"; cf. Pss. 115:3; 135:6.

In Rabbi Eliezer's retelling of the incident, the reluctance of the sailors to throw Jonah overboard is heightened. They put him in the water up to his knees and the storm stops; but when they take him out, it starts up again. Next, they put him in the water up to his navel and then to his neck; each time the storm stops but starts up again when they pull him up out of the water.[59]

15 Then they picked up Jonah and they hurled him into the sea; and the sea stopped its raging.

[12] The scene opened with the Lord hurling a big wind upon the sea (*'el-hayyām*); it closes as the sailors hurl Jonah into the sea (again, *'el-hayyām*). Jonah had said, "Pick me up and hurl me into the sea" (1:12), and now the sailors do just that. The narrator has played upon "hurl" throughout the entire scene; see on 1:4.

---

[58] The subject, "you," is before the predicate, thus receiving emphasis; see the note on 1:4.
[59] *PRE* (see Appendix, p. 106).

This time the narrator personifies the sea, as was done with the ship in 1:4: "the sea stopped its raging." Except for this instance, the verb is used for the furious anger of humans (2 Chron. 26:19; Prov. 19:12; 2 Chron. 16:10; 28:9) or of the Lord (Isa. 30:30).

With the calming of the sea, one of the points of tension driving the story reaches a preliminary resolution. The question was: What will happen to a person who tries to run away from the Lord? The answer is now clear. Consider the case of Jonah! Jonah (and anyone else who might be planning a similar "escape" from the Lord) learns that even in the uttermost parts of the sea there is no escaping the Lord (Ps. 139:9).

16 And the men feared the LORD[60] greatly; and they offered an offering to the LORD, and they vowed vows.

[16] This final statement is something of a postscript, reporting on the actions of the men on board the ship.[61] These actions are described with three cognate accusative constructions, each one progressively shorter. A literal translation reads:

> And the men feared with a great fear the LORD;
> and they offered an offering to the LORD,
> and they vowed vows.

Twice in this scene it has been reported that the sailors are afraid, first because of the storm (1:5) and then after hearing Jonah's confession (1:10). The sense of "fear" in these instances is simply to be afraid. But "fear" is also used in the Bible to denote a proper attitude of reverence and honor toward the Lord. Jonah confesses such a fear of the Lord in 1:9. Again, the narrator is playing on the various senses of one Hebrew word. This scene tells how the sailors move from terror in the face of the storm (1:5, 10) to the kind of fear of the Lord (1:16) that Jonah confesses (1:9) and that marks those rightly related to God (Mal. 3:16, "revere" twice and the passages listed at 1:9). This reverence for the Lord quickly expresses itself in action, as the sailors make offerings and vows. The words here refer to the offering of an animal sacrifice (Ex. 24:5; Lev. 22:29; Deut. 18:3; etc.). Does the statement necessarily mean that the sailors later made offerings in the temple in Jerusalem?[62] Such a sacrifice could have taken place

---

[60] There is no need to excise "the LORD" here (see *BHS*). In addition to the lack of any textual evidence, the statement is part of a climactic pattern; see p. 27 above.

[61] See the comments on structure, p. 48 n. 29.

[62] *PRE* fills in the story: "They returned to Joppa and went up to Jerusalem and circumcised the flesh of their foreskins, as it is said, 'And the men feared the Lord exceedingly; and they offered a sacrifice unto the Lord'" (Appendix, p. 107). Among modern commentators, see Stuart, 455.

aboard ship.[63] The commentators speculate on these matters; the text does not say.[64] The important thing is that these sailors, who once called upon other gods (1:5), now worship the Lord that Jonah confesses (1:9). A vow is a promise made to the Lord (Deut. 23:21–23); the contents of these promises are not indicated here. After his experience in the fish, Jonah will resolve to make sacrifices and to fulfill vows that he has made (2:9 [10]).

The story, like the sea about which it reports, has now come to a place of resting and calm. And what about Jonah? The reader or hearer of the story cannot but wonder what has happened to him. Jonah has disappeared into the sea, but this is the sea made by Jonah's God (1:9) who does as he pleases (1:15). The story is clearly one that is "to be continued."

If this is a didactic narrative, we may pause at the end of this second scene to ask what it has to teach. A good place to begin is with the statement that forms the centerpiece of the scene: "I worship the LORD, the God of heaven, who made the sea and the dry land" (1:9). With "the LORD, the God of heaven," Jonah places himself squarely in the mainstream of the Israelite theological tradition that reaches from Abraham (Gen. 24:7; cf. 24:3) to Nehemiah (Neh. 1:5). The reference to the sea and the dry land recalls similar phrases from Ps. 95:5 and Gen. 1:9–10. At the center of this scene stands the affirmation that the Lord God whom Jonah confesses is the maker of all that exists.

The narrative makes clear that the Lord is not only the maker but also the sustainer. The Lord controls the forces of nature, "hurling" a wind onto the sea as easily as a man hurls a spear (1 Sam. 18:11). The story tells how the Lord continues to work through the storm, intensifying it (1:4, 11, 13) and finally shutting it down (1:15). The reader of the New Testament cannot hear this account without thinking of another of whom it was said that "even the wind and the sea obey him" (Mark 4:41 and parallels).

The major characters in this scene are the sailors, coming from a variety of nations and representing a plurality of religious traditions. They are representatives of the people of the world and are portrayed as exemplary in every way. Over against them is Jonah, the representative of Israel, the people hearing the story, the people of God. How is he portrayed?

When in a situation of acute distress, the sailors pray and act, throwing the cargo overboard; Jonah goes to sleep. The captain asks Jonah to join in prayers aboard the storm-threatened ship; we hear no report that Jonah does so. The first time Jonah speaks is when the casting of lots has singled

---

[63] So Rudolph (p. 344); note especially the comments of Sasson to this effect (pp. 139–140).

[64] The Targum says, "and they promised to offer a sacrifice," because of the difficulty of the idea of these non-Israelites sacrificing away from the Jerusalem temple (Cathcart and Gordon, 106 and n. 29).

him out as a suspicious character. Somehow his quite correct confession of faith rings hollow, coming from one who has been neither praying nor pitching in and who in fact admits that he is on the run from his God! Gerhard von Rad once remarked that Jonah "is at his worst . . . when he talks religion in the ship's cabin."[65]

Is there something genuinely heroic in Jonah's offer to sacrifice himself for the good of the rest of the people on board? In any case, these sailors show themselves to be worthy human beings when they risk their own lives to avoid having to take the life of another (1:13). Finally, they show themselves open to theological instruction when they pray to the Lord about whom they have just been told, and they demonstrate a commendable gratitude toward the Lord when they respond to their rescue from the storm by making sacrifices and vowing vows.

What didactic purpose might this description of these non-Israelites and of Jonah have? If the story is directed to Israelites, then it is clear that their representative in the story does not come out very well. It is also clear that those sailors and their captain (1:5), later simply called "men" (1:10, 13, 16), are portrayed as admirable human beings in every way. The people of the world in this scene appear as models of piety and practicality; the representative of the people of God leaves something to be desired in both categories.

Does this narrative aim to criticize a self-centered "Jonah attitude" that from time to time crops up among those who worship the God of Israel? Does the story seek to counter a prejudiced exclusivism that may lead the people of God to believe that they have a monopoly on human virtues and an inside corner on the things of God? An exclusivism that could cause them to view the people of the world with suspicion and even refuse to share what they know and have experienced of God with those outside their own group?

Reflection on these themes calls to mind that summary of the good news which says, "God so loved the *world*" (John 3:16), including the Ninevehs and Baghdads and Calcuttas of yesterday and today. One is reminded of the story of Jesus and the woman considered an outsider (Luke 7:36–50). Or of those parables of Jesus in which the outsiders are held up before the insiders as exemplary: an outsider who proved to be a neighbor (Luke 10:25–37) and another who remembered to express thanks (Luke 17:11–19). Jesus said that he came for the sake of the outsiders, even though the insiders criticized him for doing so (Luke 15:1–2). The author of the story of Jonah would have understood.

---

[65] Von Rad, *Old Testament Theology,* 2:291.

The Fish
1:17–2:10 [2:1–11][66]

As scene II concluded, Jonah had disappeared into the waters of the Mediterranean and an eerie calm had settled on the sea. The sailors worshiped the Lord with words, acts, and in their general attitude. The story could have come to an end here, making the point that one ought not try to run away from the Lord.

But the story goes on. The Lord had initiated scene I with a word and scene II with an act. Now again, the Lord acts.

Scene III consists of a narrative introduction (1:17–2:1 [2:1–2]), a prayer (2:2–9 [3–10]), and a narrative conclusion (2:10 [11]). The chapter is framed with references to the fish, three times in 1:17–2:1 [2:1–2] and once in 2:10 [11].

1:17 [2:1] Then the LORD appointed a big fish[67] to swallow Jonah; and Jonah was in the belly of the fish three days and three nights. 2:1 [2:2] And Jonah prayed to the LORD his God from the belly of the fish.

[17 (2:1)] The Lord, who had called Jonah and who had sent the storm, acts again, this time designating a large fish to carry out a rescue operation. In the course of the narrative, the verb *mānāh,* "assign, appoint," appears four times, each time with a different name for God as subject. The Lord (*Yahweh*) appoints a fish (1:17), the Lord God (*Yahweh elohim*) appoints a plant (4:6), the God (*ha elohim*) appoints a worm (4:7), and God (*elohim*) appoints a wind (4:8). When the emphasis is on the gracious and beneficial action of God, the name *Yahweh* is used. When the emphasis is on God's disciplining action, *elohim* appears; *Yahweh elohim* makes the transition from the one to the other.[68] As easily as a king *appoints* a particular diet (Dan. 1:10) or as an official in the palace *appoints* a guard (Dan. 1:11), so the Lord orders the creatures and forces of nature. "Wisdom thinking," says Wolff, "has made this theologian familiar with Yahweh's playful dealings with his creatures (Prov. 8:30–31)."[69]

---

[66] The Hebrew verse numbers are given in brackets.

[67] "Fish" occurs four times in the book. In three instances the Hebrew is the masculine noun *dāg* (1:17 [2:1] twice; 2:10 [11]), while in 2:1 [2] the Hebrew is the feminine *dāgāh.* The GKC grammar (122s,t) states that while feminine forms are often used for collectives (cf. the construct form of *dāgāh* in Gen. 1:26), this is an exception, a *nomen unitatis* referring to a single fish.

The *Midrash Jonah* explains the two forms by introducing a pregnant female fish into the story; see Appendix, p. 110. A less imaginative but more likely explanation would understand this variation in forms as a stylistic device, seeking to avoid too many repetitions of the same word in the same place; see the comments of Sasson, 155–157.

[68] See "The Names for God in Jonah," pp. 45–46 above; and Magonet, *Form,* 33–38.

[69] Wolff, *Obadiah and Jonah,* 132.

What sort of "big fish" did the author have in mind here? The Greek translations have *kētei megalō* (*kētous* in Matt. 12:40) which may be translated "great sea monster,"[70] while the Vulgate translates *piscem grandem,* "big fish." The Hebrew "big fish" (the seventh of fourteen occurrences of *gādôl,* "big," in the story) does not denote a specific species but leaves room for the imagination of the hearer or reader.[71] A prayer of the priest Eleazar in a work from the first century B.C. recalls some of the great acts of the Lord's deliverance: the exodus, the retreat of Sennacherib, the three men in the furnace, Daniel, and then Jonah.[72] The priest reveals his impression of the creature:

> And Jonah, wasting away in the belly of a huge, sea-born monster, you, Father, watched over and restored unharmed to all his family.
> (3 Macc. 6:8)

Writing near the end of the first century A.D., Josephus introduces the incident with reserve, if not skepticism: "It is also related that Jonah was swallowed down by a whale, and that when he had been there three days, and as many nights, he was vomited out upon the Euxine Sea, and this alive, and without any hurt upon his body."[73]

The story about Jonah and the whale or sea monster has called forth an amazing number and variety of artistic representations. In a manner appropriate to the broad range of possibilities given by the Hebrew "big fish," that creature has been depicted in forms ranging from the serpentlike monster found on a fourth-century A.D. Christian sarcophagus in Rome[74] and the piglike animal depicted in ivory sculptures from Asia Minor[75] to ferocious or friendly-looking whales in painting, sketches, sculpture, or stained glass.[76] One of the most memorable representations is in a baroque church in Duszniki Zdroj in southwestern Poland, where the pulpit is in

---

[70] BAGD[2], 431; NRSV "sea monster" in Matt. 12:40.

[71] Wolff (*Studien,* 20–28) surveys a number of ancient texts that report the swallowing of a hero by a sea monster, including sun and moon myths, Greek sagas of Heracles or Perseus, a variant of the Jason saga, the story of Arion's rescue by a dolphin, stories from ancient India, and a variation of the Perseus-Andromeda tradition located in Joppa. For a thorough discussion of these themes, see Steffen, *Mysterium,* part 2; see also Komlos, "Jonah Legends."

[72] Note also the sequence in the *Hellenistic Synagogal Prayers* (between A.D. 150 and 350): "Daniel in the hole of the lions; Jonah in the belly of the whale; the three children in a furnace of fire" (*OTP,* 2:684–685); see Appendix for both texts.

[73] *Antiquities* 10; see Appendix for the complete text.

[74] For an illustration, see Steffen, *Mysterium, Tafel* V.

[75] For an illustration, see the cover of *Bible Review* 6 (August 1990).

[76] For some illustrations and discussion, see Limburg, "Jonah and the Whale," *Bible Review* 6 (August 1990): 18–25; the issue also includes a number of other Jonah photographs. See also Vanoni, Steffen, et al., "Jona als Typ unsterblich," *Bibel heute* 27 (1991, 1st quarter); and see the works by Steffen cited in the bibliography.

the form of a whale. The preacher stands in the mouth of the creature, directly below a row of huge teeth. The tail makes a loop and curls up the wall behind the pulpit.[77]

The word "swallow" carries a sense of suddenness. Samaria will be swallowed (NRSV "eats it up") as quickly as one gulps down the first ripe fig of the season (Isa. 28:4); the Kohathites are not to look on the holy things even "for a moment" (NRSV), literally, "for a swallow" (Num. 4:20). Just as Aaron's snake gulped down those of the Egyptian magicians (Ex. 7:12) or as the earth swallowed up the wicked family of Korah (Num. 16:30–34; Deut. 11:6; Ps. 106:17), so the big fish swallows Jonah.

The language here and in 2:10 [11] is that of eating and disgorging food. The same vocabulary occurs in Job 20, where Zophar says of the wicked, "Their food is turned in their *stomachs*. . . . *They swallow* down riches and *vomit* them up again" (Job 20:14–15). The big fish *swallows* Jonah, who is in the fish's *stomach;* after three days he will be *vomited* up again (2:10 [11]). The Hebrew word translated "belly" is not used with anatomical precision. It may have the sense "womb" (Gen. 25:23) or "entrails" (2 Sam. 20:10), or it may denote the place where the heart is located (Ps. 22:14 [15], NRSV "breast") or even where teaching is stored up (Ps. 40:8, NRSV "heart").

The only other place in the Old Testament where "three days and three nights" occurs is 1 Sam. 30:12, where it is reported of an Egyptian found lying unconscious in the open country that "he had not eaten bread or drunk water for three days and three nights." In the course of Jonah's story, this is the period of time needed for the great fish to reach the place where Jonah is to be disgorged.

Some later Jewish interpretations describe Jonah's stay in the fish in imaginative detail. According to the *Pirke de Rabbi Eliezer,* Jonah saves his host fish from being devoured by the monster Leviathan. In return for this, the fish takes Jonah on an extensive tour of the suboceanic world. In the *Zohar,* Jonah's sojourn in the belly of the fish and his subsequent ejection is understood as an allegory of death and resurrection. Most interesting is the account in *Midrash Jonah,* apparently developed to account for the variation between the masculine and feminine words for fish in these verses. Jonah found himself quite comfortable in the big fish, was not worried, and failed to pray. Then the Lord arranges for Jonah to be spit out of the original (male) fish (1:17 [2:1], Heb., *dāg,* masc.) and to be swallowed by another (female) fish (2:1 [2:2] *dāgāh,* fem.) that is

---

[77] For discussion and illustrations, see Steffen, *Mysterium,* 136; and G. Grundmann, *Barocke Kirchen und Klöster in Schlesien* (Munich: Bergstadtverlag Wilh. Gottl. Korn, 1971²), 20, 126–127.

pregnant with 365,000 baby fish in its womb. In this situation Jonah was "very much afraid because of the dirt and refuse from all the fish" and immediately began to pray.[78]

Aldous Huxley has pictured the scene with imagination:

> Seated upon the convex mound
> Of one vast kidney, Jonah prays
> And sings his canticles and hymns,
> Making the hollow vault resound
> God's goodness and mysterious ways,
> Till the great fish spouts music as he swims.[79]

[2:1 (2)] The identical verb form "prayed" occurs in 4:2, where it introduces Jonah's bitter complaint to the Lord. The verb "prayed" can designate praying for help in a situation of acute distress (1 Sam. 1:10; 2 Kings 4:33; 6:18; 20:2), or it can introduce a psalm of thanksgiving, as in 1 Sam. 2:1 and here.

[2:2-9 (3-10)] The prayer is built on the pattern of the psalm of individual thanksgiving and is to a great degree made up of phrases from the psalms. Vocabulary duplicated in the Psalter is underlined.

2[3] I called to the LORD out of my distress,
          and he answered me;[80]
       from the innermost part of Sheol I cried,[81]
          you heard my voice.[82]
3[4] For you cast me[83] into the deep,[84]
          into the heart of the sea,[85]
          and the flood surrounded me.
       All your breakers and your waves passed over me.[86]
4[5] And as for me, I said,
          "I have been driven away from before your eyes;[87]

---

[78] For these texts, see Appendix.

[79] "Jonah," in *The Cherry Tree: A Collection of Poems,* ed. G. Grigson (New York: Vanguard Press, 1959), 211.

[80] Ps. 120:1; the vocabulary is the same but the word order is different: "To the Lord in my distress I called and he answered me."

[81] Ps. 30:2 [3].

[82] "You heard voice . . . my cry," Ps. 31:22.

[83] "For you cast me/have . . . thrown me," Ps. 102:10 [11].

[84] Ps. 69:2 [3], 15 [16].

[85] *BHS* suggests deleting either "deep" or "into the heart of the sea" apparently to preserve the 3 + 2 meter of the psalm. But this is unnecessary. Rudolph (p. 346 n. 4) points out that even in Lamentations, where this 3 + 2 or *qinah* pattern occurs extensively, there are breaks in the pattern. See Sasson (pp. 173-175), who retains the MT.

[86] Ps. 42:7 [8].

[87] Ps. 31:22 [23].

how[88] shall I again look at your holy temple?"[89]

5[6]   Water[90] closed in on me[91] up to my neck,
        the deep surrounded me;
        weeds were wrapped around my head.

6[7]   I went down to the bottom of the mountains,[92]
        the land whose bars shut me in forever;
        and you brought my life up from the Pit,[93] LORD my God.

7[8]   As my life was slipping away,[94]
        I remembered[95] the LORD;
        and my prayer came to you,[96]
        to your holy temple.[97]

8[9]   Those who worship worthless idols[98]
        abandon the one who loves them.[99]

9[10]   But as for me, with a song of thanksgiving
        I will make offerings[100] to you,
        what I have vowed I will fulfill;[101]
        Deliverance is from the LORD![102]

EXCURSUS: THE SONG OF THANKSGIVING

Jonah's prayer identifies itself as a "song of thanksgiving" (Heb., *tôdāh,* 2:9 [10]; cf. Ps. 116:17) and is best understood in the context of psalms of this type.[103] Included in this category are Psalms 18; 30; 32; 34; 40:1–10;

---

[88] Reading *'êk,* "how," with the *BHS* proposal instead of MT *'ak,* "surely," because of the parallelism; Theodotion has *pōs,* "how." Sasson retains the MT, translating, "Driven from your sight, may I yet continue to gaze toward your holy sanctuary"; see his discussion in *Jonah,* 179–180.

[89] Pss. 5:7 [8]; 138:2.

[90] "Water . . . up to my neck," Ps. 69:1 [2].

[91] "Encompassed me," Pss. 18:4 [5]; 116:3.

[92] The emendation and rearrangement proposed in *BHS* is not necessary; see the comments of Sasson, 185–187.

[93] Ps. 103:4.

[94] "When my spirit is faint," Ps. 142:3 [4]; cf. Ps. 143:4 [5].

[95] Ps. 143:5 [6].

[96] Ps. 88:2 [3]; "it came to you," Ps. 102:1 [2].

[97] Pss. 5:7 [8]; 138:2.

[98] Ps. 31:6 [7]; the proposed emendation in *BHS* is not necessary; see Sasson, 196–197.

[99] Lit., "abandon their *hesed* = steadfast love," i.e., the one who shows steadfast love to them.

[100] "I will make offerings . . . thanksgiving," Ps. 116:17.

[101] Pss. 22:25 [26]; 116:18.

[102] Ps. 3:8 [9].

[103] For a discussion of the Individual Song of Thanksgiving, see F. Crüsemann, *Studien*

66:13-20; 92; 116; 118; and 138. These psalms articulate the psalmist's grateful response to God for a specific act of deliverance, such as healing from illness (Pss. 30; 32; 116), deliverance from enemies (Pss. 18; 92; 118; 138), or simply rescue from trouble (Ps. 66:14). They assume the presence of the congregation gathered for worship (Pss. 30:4–5; 34:5, 8, 9; 118:1–4, 24, 29) or for instruction (Pss. 32:8–11; 34:11–14) and tell the story of the deliverance that has been experienced (Pss. 40:9–10; 66:16–19). These psalms contain hints that point to the way in which they were used in worship: there may have been a procession (Ps. 118:19–29) or a thank offering accompanying the psalms (Pss. 66:13–15; 116:12–19). Psalm 138:2 assumes that the worshiper is in the outer court of the temple. At the heart of these psalms is the *story of the deliverance,* summarized briefly (Pss. 18:3; 30:2; 34:4, 6; 40:1–2; 66:19; 92:4; 116:1–2; 118:5; 138:3) and often expanded (Pss. 18:4–19, 31–45; 30:6–11; 32:3–5; 66:16–19; 92:10–11; 116:3–4, 6–9, 16; 118:10–18). The verbal cognate of *tôdāh* is *yādāh,* which occurs frequently in these psalms and is translated in a variety of ways: "extol" (Ps. 18:49); "give thanks" (Ps. 30:4); "praise" (Pss. 30:9; 138:4); "confess" (Ps. 32:5); "give thanks" or "thank" (Pss. 30:12; 92:1; 118:1, 19, 21, 28, 29; 138:1, 2).[104]

A comparison of this prayer in Jonah with Psalm 30 as an example of the "Song of Thanksgiving" is instructive:

	Psalm 30	Jonah 2
Brief summary of distress, deliverance	vs. 1–3	vs. 2, 7
Word to congregation	vs. 4–5	vs. 2a, 7a, 8, 9b
Description of distress	vs. 6–10	vs. 3–6a
Deliverance	v. 11	v. 6b
Vow to praise	v. 12	v. 9a

In Psalm 30, vs. 4–5 speak to the congregation *about* the Lord, calling them to praise (v. 4) and giving a reason for praise (v. 5). The remainder of the psalm is addressed *to* the Lord. The alternation between speech addressed to the Lord and speech about the Lord is explained by the use of the psalm in the context of congregational worship.

---

zur Formgeschichte von Hymnus und Danklied in Israel, WMANT 32 (Neukirchen-Vluyn: Neukirchener Verlag, 1969), esp. 247–249. See also C. Westermann, *The Psalms: Structure, Content and Message,* trans. R. D. Gehrke (Minneapolis: Augsburg Publishing House, 1980), 71–80; idem, *Praise and Lament,* trans. K. Crim and R. N. Soulen (Atlanta: John Knox Press, 1981), 25–30; and idem, *The Living Psalms,* trans. J. R. Porter (Grand Rapids: Wm. B. Eerdmans Publishing House, 1989), 122–123.

[104] Westermann has argued that the verb *yādāh* should be translated "praise" and on this basis prefers to classify these psalms as "narrative praise of the individual" (*Praise and Lament,* 25–30; and *The Living Psalms,* 166–167 [n. 103 above]).

This same distinction may be observed in the Jonah psalm. While most of the psalm speaks *to* the Lord, statements *about* the Lord are made in 2:2a, 7a, 9b, and, indirectly, 8 ("the one who loves them"). These statements assume the presence of a listening congregation and thus point to the use of the psalm and of the entire book of Jonah in the context of a gathered community. Consideration of these statements *about* the Lord provides an important clue to the preaching and teaching aim of the psalm and of the book as a whole.

[2 (3)] This verse is a *brief summary* of the story told in the psalm, first in I/Lord language that speaks words of witness about the Lord to the congregation and then in I/you language addressed to the Lord. The "story" may be followed by noting the first-person verbs: "I called . . . I cried (2:2) . . . I said . . . I have been driven away (2:4) . . . I went down (2:6) . . . I remembered (2:7) . . . I will make offerings (2:9) . . . I have vowed, I will fulfill (2:9)." Jonah's prayer is formulated in the traditional language of the psalms and other biblical prayers; see the underlined portions in the translation.[105]

"Called" recalls the captain's request that Jonah call upon his God (1:6); now Jonah finally carries out the request. The word has already come up at other points in the story: Jonah was told to call/preach against Nineveh (1:2) and the sailors called/cried out to the Lord before throwing Jonah overboard (1:14). "Distress" is a word frequently found in the psalms, translated as "trouble, troubles" (Pss. 22:11 [12]; 25:17; 34:17) or "adversities" (Ps. 31:7). It may refer to distress resulting from a past action (Gen. 42:21) or to the anguish of a woman giving birth (Jer. 4:31; 49:24) or to the distress of the whole community at the time of the fall of Jerusalem (Obad. 12, 14).

The expression "innermost part of Sheol" occurs only here in the Bible (cf. Prov. 18:8; 22:18). Sheol is the place where people go at death (Gen. 37:35; 44:31; Ps. 88:3). It is located under the earth (Num. 16:30–33). Residence there is permanent (Job 7:9–10), with bars (Job 17:16) or cords (Pss. 18:5; 49:15) preventing escape. The word can be used synonymously with death (Pss. 6:5; 18:5; Isa. 28:15, 18; 38:18). Sheol may be personified and described as hungry and greedy (Isa. 5:14; Hab. 2:5) and never satisfied (Prov. 27:20; 30:16). It is a place of darkness (Job 17:13) where there is

---

[105] Cf. the comment of Keil: "The prayer consists for the most part of reminiscences of passages in the Psalms, which were so exactly suited to Jonah's circumstances, that he could not have expressed his thoughts and feelings any better in words of his own" (*Biblical Commentary on the OT,* vol. 1: *The 12 Minor Prophets* [Edinburgh: T. & T. Clark, 1871], 399).

no work or wisdom or thought (Eccl. 9:10). In Sheol there is neither praise of God nor telling of God's love (Pss. 6:5; 88:11; Isa. 38:18), nor are the acts of God remembered (Ps. 88:10–12). The psalmist can even say that those who are in Sheol are forgotten, cut off from the Lord's hand (Ps. 88:5). However, Sheol is still not out of the range of the Lord (Ps. 139:8; Hos. 13:14; Amos 9:2). God sees what is happening even there (Job 25:6; Prov. 15:11) and will not abandon his own who reside there (Ps. 49:15).

"Cried" refers to those in desperate need. Again, the word is frequent in the psalms (Pss. 5:2; 18:6; 22:24; etc.) and in Job (Job 19:7; 24:12; 29:12; etc.) and can even be used for the young raven's cry to God for food (Job 38:41). "You heard my voice" is also typical psalm language (Pss. 31:22; 116:1).

[3–6a] These verses provide a *description of the distress* in narrative form, Jonah telling of his experience after being thrown overboard:

[3 (4)] Jonah holds the Lord responsible for his being "cast" into "the deep"; cf. Ps. 102:10 and 2 Kings 2:16. Just as the Lord deals with sins by casting them into the deep (Micah 7:19), so, says Jonah, the Lord has dealt with him. "The deep" refers literally to the sea (Pss. 68:22; 107:24; Micah 7:19) or is often used figuratively for distress (Pss. 69:2, 15; 88:6). The "heart of" is the inner or central part; cf. "heart of heaven" in Deut. 4:11. The words "all your breakers and your waves" also occur in Ps. 42:7b as a metaphor for extreme distress; cf. also 2 Sam. 22:5. The doubled "your" assigns the responsibility for Jonah's plight to the Lord. The Targum tones down the harshness of this notion, reading here, "All the gales of the sea and its billows passed over me."[106] The Lord has made the sea (1:9) and it is under his control.

[4 (5)] The translation "as for me" seeks to catch the emphasis in the Hebrew on the subject "I."[107] Just as the sea is driven by the wind (Isa. 57:20) or the Nile is tossed about by the forces of nature (Amos 8:8), so Jonah feels himself "driven away" from the Lord's sight by forces he cannot control. The last lines continue the "sight" theme. Jonah says in effect: "I have been driven away from your eyes, Lord; and how will my eyes ever again see your temple?" If he ever escapes, Jonah vows to give thanks and to sacrifice to the Lord, presumably in the "holy temple" in Jerusalem (2:9; cf. Ps. 79:1). Psalm 138 presents the sort of prayer that an individual might use to give thanks on such an occasion.

[5 (6)] With "closed in on me," the prayer continues to use traditional language: 2 Sam. 22:5; Pss. 18:4 [5]; 116:3. The expression "water . . . to my neck" also occurs in Ps. 69:1 [2]. The Hebrew translated "neck" is *nepeš*,

---

106 Cathcart and Gordon, 107.
107 See note 30 on 1:4.

which can also mean "life"; see the comments on the word in 2:7 below. The Targum is more abstract: "unto death."[108]

Up to this point in Jonah's prayer, the language has been that of traditional biblical prayer, as is evident from the underlined portions in the translation above. Now, however, beginning with "the deep" (2:5) and continuing through "forever" (2:6), "the language is uniquely that of Jonah with no echo elsewhere. Jonah's descent from conventional experience is matched by a move beyond conventional language."[109]

The word translated "weeds" is also used for the reeds where the baby Moses was hidden (Ex. 2:3, 5) and for the reeds in the Nile (Isa. 19:6). Outside these three passages, it is found in the combination "sea of reeds." The weeds are "wrapped" around Jonah's head, just as one ties a headdress on one's head (Ex. 29:9; Lev. 8:13). The Targum has, "The Red Sea was suspended above my head."[110]

[6 (7)] The picture is that of a person going down into the depths of the sea and facing death. With "I went down," the sequence of Jonah's "going down" is complete (1:3 twice, 5). Both his horizontal and his vertical distance from the Lord are at the maximum. "Bars" were part of the security equipment of the city gates (Deut. 3:5; Neh. 3:3, 6), made of bronze (1 Kings 4:13) or iron (Isa. 45:2). Jonah was completely trapped, locked up in the inner recesses of the earth. With "forever," Jonah's description of his distressful situation is concluded.

The prayer describes the *deliverance* that Jonah experienced in v. 6b. "And you brought my life up" marks a return to traditional biblical language (Ps. 103:4). "The Pit" is the place where one goes at death (Isa. 51:14; Ps. 30:9) and may be used synonymously with Sheol (Ps. 16:10). One who lives forever would never see the Pit (Ps. 49:9; NRSV "grave"). A violent death "in the heart of the seas" (cf. Jonah 2:3 [4]) means being thrust down to the Pit (Ezek. 28:8). A rescue from death means being saved from the Pit (Job 33:28; Ps. 103:4). Jonah addresses God as "Lord my God"; see also 1:9. For a discussion of the variety of names for God in Jonah, see pp. 45–46 above.

[7 (8)] Here is another *brief summary* of Jonah's distress and deliverance, completing the frame around the narrative account (cf. 2:2 [3]). The first half of the verse is a *word to the congregation,* Jonah telling about his experience. Once again, a testimony about the Lord is followed by I/you language addressed to the Lord (cf. 2:2 [3]).

The use of traditional language continues with "As my life was slipping away, I remembered" (Pss. 142:3 [4]; 143:4 [5]). The Hebrew word for

---

[108] Cathcart and Gordon, 107.
[109] Magonet, "Jonah, Book of," *ABD* 3:936–942; see also his comments in *Form,* 49.
[110] Cathcart and Gordon, 107.

"life" is *nepeš,* which has a variety of meanings: (1) In 2:5 [6], the word is used in its most basic, concrete sense: "The waters came up to my *nepeš* = neck" (cf. Ps. 69:1 [2]). (2) The word can also denote "breath." It is said of the monster Leviathan that "his breath (*nepeš*) kindles coals" (Job 41:21 [12]). This breath is the life force itself, breathed into animals and human creatures by the Lord at the time of creation (Gen. 1:20, 24, 30; 2:7). (3) Then *nepeš* can also be used to denote the entire human person. It may substitute for the personal pronoun: "Let me die [lit., "let my *nepeš* die"] the death of the upright" (Num. 23:10; cf. Deut. 4:9, RSV). This is the sense here: "As my life (*nepeš*) was slipping away." The same vocabulary appears in Psalm 107, in a description of those near death in the desert: "hungry and thirsty, their life (*nepeš*) was slipping away within them" (Ps. 107:5).

Jonah's prayer continues with "I remembered the LORD." In Psalm 42, a psalmist far from the temple and remembering the joys of worship with the community (Ps. 42:4) finds himself depressed and discouraged (Ps. 42:5). Like a deer that longs for water, he says, "so my soul (*nepeš*) longs for you, O God. My soul (*nepeš*) thirsts for God" (Ps. 42:1-2). He even speaks metaphorically of the Lord's waves rolling over him (Ps. 42:7b; cf. Jonah 2:3b [4b]). In this situation he says to the Lord, "therefore I remember you" (Ps. 42:6). The context in Jonah is similar. Jonah is far away from the worshiping community, his *nepeš* is slipping away, and he thinks about "your holy temple." According to 2:2, Jonah prayed in the words of this psalm; here Jonah recalls that his prayer had been heard: "and my prayer came to you." The "holy temple" plays an important part in this prayer. Jonah had thought that he would never see it again (2:4 [5]). But now, looking back at his near-death experience in the stormy sea, he realizes that his prayer reached the Lord in the Lord's temple.

[8 (9)]   After the strong I/you language that marks most of this psalm, this sentence stands out as a *word to the congregation,* almost as a maxim or motto, with a clear didactic intent.

The sense of the Hebrew *hablê,* translated as "idols," from the noun *hebel,* is illuminated by two texts where the word is used in parallelism. The parallel in Jer. 8:19 is "images"; the parallel in Deut. 32:21 is "what is no god." Thus *hebel* here appears to refer to idols, intensified with "worthless." Psalm 31:6 is the only other instance where this same expression occurs: "I hate those paying regard to worthless idols, but I trust in the LORD." The meaning of the expression is the opposite of trusting in the Lord — in other words, putting trust in idols.

The word "abandon" may be used for a doe forsaking a fawn (Jer. 14:5), parents forsaking a child (Ps. 27:10), or a wife leaving a husband (Prov. 2:17). The word is often used in connection with forsaking the true God for the worship of other gods (Judg. 10:10; Deut. 31:20; Jer. 1:16). Those who rely on idols are abandoning "their steadfast love," that is, the one who loves them steadfastly, or God.

The Hebrew word behind "loves" is *ḥesed*. On the human level, this is the kind of love/loyalty that exists between two individuals who have made a covenant with each other. Thus David and Jonathan have made a covenant (1 Sam. 20:8) and that covenant relationship is marked by love/loyalty (1 Sam. 20:14, "loyal love," and v. 15, "loyalty," both of which translate *ḥesed*). The word may be used of human love/loyalty toward God (Hos. 6:4, 6). Most often, *ḥesed* refers to God's enduring love toward humans (Pss. 100:5; 106:1; 107:1; 118:1–2; 136:1–26). In Jonah 4:2, "steadfast love" (*ḥesed*) is listed among the qualities of God. Here also the word refers to God's love, willfully abandoned by those who choose to pay regard to idols.

Verse 8 [9] is one of the few clues in the book that reveal something about the audience that is being addressed. These are people who are putting their trust in some form of religion involving idol worship and are thus abandoning the God who rescued Jonah in this dramatic way.

[9 (10)] Jonah's prayer comes to an end with the *vow to praise*.

As in 2:4 [5], the pronoun is emphasized, here set in contrast to the statement before, "But as for me." Rather than abandoning the Lord, the source of love, Jonah declares that he will give thanks and offer sacrifice.

The literal Hebrew behind "song of thanksgiving" is "sound of thanksgiving" (*beqôl tôdāh*). Since *tôdāh* is often used in parallel with song (Ps. 69:30) or singing (Ps. 95:2) and since it occurs with verbs denoting singing (Neh. 12:27; Isa. 51:3; Ps. 147:7), the sense here appears to be songs accompanying the making of a sacrifice. Jonah's prayer ends with a promise to offer sacrifices and to pay vows. The thank offering or *tôdāh* would be appropriate after a deliverance such as this (cf. Pss. 50:14; 107:22; 116:17). In the sacrificial system, the *tôdāh* is a subdivision of the peace offering. It was accompanied by animal sacrifice and a cereal offering (Lev. 7:11–18). For the promise to pay vows, coupled with the making of an offering, see Ps. 66:13–15; see also 2 Sam. 15:7; Pss. 22:25; 50:14; 56:12; 116:14, 18. The reference to the "song of thanksgiving" here may indicate that actual sacrifices have been replaced by offerings in the form of verbal praise.[111]

The final *word to the congregation* in the song is, "Deliverance is from the LORD." The Masoretic tradition called attention to this two-word

---

[111] See H.-J. Kraus, *Psalms 60–150* (Minneapolis: Augsburg Publishing House, 1989), on Ps. 116:17; and the comments of Crüsemann (note 103 above), 248.

statement in Hebrew by framing it with strong disjunctive marks (the *'atnāḥ* under "I will fulfill" and the *sillûq* and *sôp pāsûq* after "from the LORD"). In addition, the first Masoretic paragraph marker in the book, the *setumah,* comes after this sentence.[112] If the theological significance of scene II (1:4–16) came to focus in the confession in 1:9 with its declaration about God who creates, the theological center of this scene is most clearly expressed in this statement that God delivers, rescues, saves those who call upon God in a time of trouble.[113]

10[11] Then the LORD spoke to the fish, and it vomited Jonah out onto the dry land.

[10 (11)] This brief statement completes the narrative framework and brings the scene to a close. The scene opened with the Lord appointing a fish. It closes as the Lord speaks to the fish and the fish responds. The verb "vomited" is used literally in only two other biblical texts, Prov. 23:8 and 25:16; cf. the cognate noun in Prov. 26:11. The Lord speaks, the fish vomits, and Jonah is sitting on the "dry land," which he knew the Lord had made (1:9) and which, just a few days before, his ship had not been able to reach (1:13).

What is of theological interest in this chapter, considered as a whole?

The narrative framework to the prayer (1:17–2:1 plus 2:10) may be regarded as an exposition of Jonah's confessional statement in 1:9. That statement spoke of the Lord "who made the sea and the dry land," and the entire second scene (1:4–16) demonstrated in dramatic form God's continued involvement in controlling nature. Scene III now provides another illustration of God's continued involvement in the natural world. Having sent a storm and then stopped it, the Lord orders one of the largest creatures in the sea to swallow Jonah, then to swim with him for a number of days, and finally to spit him up onto the beach. In sum, God the creator continues to control events in the natural world.

Considering Jonah's prayer within the context of the book as a whole helps one understand how the completed book functioned in the worship life of ancient Israel and also provides some directives suggesting how it might continue to address believing communities today. As a typical "Song of Thanksgiving" (2:9) the prayer speaks to the Lord but also includes words of witness directed toward a listening community. These words, in 2:2a,

---

[112] The Dead Sea Scroll text of Jonah also indicates a break here, leaving a blank line after v. 9 [10]; DJD, 2:191.

[113] Claus Westermann has called attention to these two basic shapes of God's activity, creating/blessing and delivering; see his *Elements of Old Testament Theology* (Atlanta: John Knox Press, 1982).

7a, 8, and 9b, all speak to the congregation *about* the Lord and thus bring the theological and didactic intent of the chapter into sharp focus.

The first of these words in 2:2a is presented as Jonah's testimony to those hearing the story and the song. In the traditional language of Israelite prayer, these words address those who themselves are experiencing distress, anguish, and trouble and provide a model for what to do in such straits: "I called to the LORD out of my distress, and he answered me." Those who find themselves *in extremis,* who may be facing a moment that will make the difference between life and death, can further identify with the words of 2:7a: "As my life was slipping away, I remembered the LORD."

The final words of the song capture the essence of that which the chapter teaches, in the form of a motto: "Deliverance is from the LORD" (2:9b). The Hebrew word for "deliverance" here is *yešû'ātāh,* from *yešû'āh.* When the angel announced to Mary that she would have a son, the angel said, "You shall call his name Jesus [Heb., *yešû'āh*], for he will save his people from their sins" (Matt. 1:21). The Christian reader who hears this conclusion to Jonah's prayer in its original language cannot miss this word that sounds so much like the Hebrew name of Jesus, which has meant deliverance and salvation for the peoples of the world (John 3:16).

There is yet another of these statements that speak *about* God. This one is the most explicitly didactic comment in the book: Those who rely on worthless idols abandon the one who loves them (2:8). Here is an exposition of the most basic of the commandments: "You shall have no other gods before me" (Ex. 20:2–3). This warning against idolatry is addressed to those tempted to substitute some other religion for the biblical faith. To do so, says this word, would be like a child forsaking a loving parent, or a husband or wife abandoning a loving spouse. This would be nothing less than throwing away the steadfast and loyal love of God and replacing it with an empty pseudoreligion.

EXCURSUS: THE SIGN OF JONAH

Jonah is mentioned three times in the New Testament, in each case in connection with "the sign of Jonah."

1. Matthew 12:38–42 refers to the whole Jonah story with its two major parts, the incident with the fish and the preaching in Nineveh. Jesus does not retell the story but assumes that his hearers are familiar with it. Jonah is named "the prophet Jonah," recalling that designation in 2 Kings 14:25.

On other occasions when the Pharisees are seeking a sign, they are said to be "testing" Jesus and the context is clearly an argumentative one (Matt. 16:1; Mark 8:11). Despite the respectful address, "Teacher," it seems that here again the relationship between questioners and the one questioned is tense, since Jesus immediately associates looking for signs with "an evil and adulterous generation."

The central point of this pericope is the parallel and alliterative statement in Matt. 12:40:

> For just as Jonah was in the belly (*koilia*) of the sea monster
> three days and three nights,
> so will the Son of Man be in the heart (*kardia*) of the earth
> three days and three nights.

The "sign of Jonah" refers to the near-death/deliverance experience of the prophet, here understood as a prefiguring of the death and deliverance of Jesus.

The pericope concludes with two examples of how people ought to respond when a Jonah-like figure is among them. Jesus is addressing a group of men, some of them experts in interpreting Jewish tradition (scribes) and some of them members of the party of the Pharisees. These representatives of the best in Judaism could learn something, says Jesus, from certain non-Jewish people! The Ninevites heard Jonah's preaching and repented. Those hearing Jesus ought to do the same, because the person and proclamation of Jesus is something greater than Jonah! Furthermore, suggests Jesus, these Jewish men gathered before him could learn from a non-Jewish woman. The "queen of the South" (the queen of Sheba, 1 Kings 10) put great value on Solomon's wisdom. These people who call Jesus "Teacher" should react in the same way to the words of Jesus, because the wisdom of Jesus is greater than that of Solomon!

2. Matthew 16:1–4 makes reference to the sign of Jonah without explaining it; the explanation has been given in Matthew 12. "You Pharisees and Sadducees can explain the signs in nature," Jesus says here, "but you don't understand the signs of the momentous times (*kairoi*) when we are living." One sign will be given to this generation, that to which the "sign of Jonah" pointed (Matt. 12:40): the death and resurrection of Jesus.

3. The discussion about the sign of Jonah in Luke 11:29–32 is shorter than that of Matthew 12 and its meaning is not as obvious. Instead of carrying on a dialogue with Pharisees, Jesus is addressing a crowd. "An evil generation seeks a sign," he says, "but no sign shall be given it but the sign of Jonah."

This time the sign of Jonah is not so immediately identifiable. "For just as Jonah became a sign to the people of Nineveh, so the Son of man will be to this generation" (Luke 11:30). In what way was Jonah a "sign" to the people of Nineveh? The most natural explanation is that Jonah told them of his near-death/deliverance experience. In the same way, the Son of man's death and resurrection will be a sign pointing to God's power.

In Luke's version, the Gentile woman who was a queen is held up as the first example. She, a non-Jew and a woman, valued Solomon's wisdom; so this audience ought to value the wisdom of Jesus, who is greater than Solomon! Finally, the Gentiles in Nineveh are again cited as an example of how people ought to respond to the message of a prophet. They repented! If they, a foreign people, responded in this way to the preaching of Jonah, how much more the people of Jesus' day ought to respond to his proclamation — because Jesus is greater than Jonah!

These texts which put the experience of Jonah alongside the death and resurrection of Jesus have received dramatic exposition at the hands of a number of artists. In a magnificent stained-glass window in the Cologne Cathedral in Germany, a series of Old Testament and New Testament scenes are juxtaposed. Among these is a colorful Jonah, escaping from the jaws of a fierce sea monster with a double spout of water emerging from his snout. Next to this is Jesus emerging from the tomb, unnoticed by two sleeping guards.[114]

An even more remarkable illustration of this text is the huge Jonah window in St. John's church in Gouda, the Netherlands. Among the seventy stained-glass windows, some more than sixty feet high, is one of Jonah emerging from a monstrous fish. In the background one sees storm clouds and the ship, with Jonah being thrown overboard. In the foreground is a mighty mouth and part of a large blue eye. The prophet, clothed in yellow, red, and blue, is striding out of the fish's mouth. His body language suggests determination; his clothing, action. His eyes look at the beholder with a glimmer of humor in his expression and his finger points to a banner he is carrying with the slogan in Latin, "Behold, something greater than Jonah is here."[115]

The Reassignment
3:1-3a

Since Jonah has promised to offer sacrifices and fulfill vows (2:9), we might expect the narrative to continue with an account of a visit to the temple in Jerusalem where those activities could be carried out.

This scene, however, brings a surprise. We are suddenly taken back to the beginning of the story. Again, the Lord initiates the action by giving Jonah his original assignment once more (3:1-2). This time Jonah begins

---

[114] For photographs, see *Bible Review* 6 (August 1990): 22-23.
[115] For a photograph, see again *Bible Review* 6 (August 1990): 19.

to carry it out (3:3a). The scene is framed by the inclusio, "word of the LORD."

3:1 Then the word of the LORD came to Jonah a second time, saying, 2 "Get up, go to Nineveh, that great city, and proclaim to it the proclamation that I am telling you." 3a So Jonah got up and went to Nineveh, according to the word of the LORD.

"Now that is more like it" is the immediate reaction of anyone who is familiar with biblical stories about prophets. These accounts often begin with a command to "Get up and go" and continue by reporting that the prophet got up and went (1 Kings 17:8-10; 2 Kings 1:15-16). The story of Jonah seems to be back on track. The prophet goes to Nineveh.

[3:1] The words are identical to 1:1 except for "a second time" which takes the place of "son of Amittai." This formula introducing a second word from the Lord also occurs in Jer. 1:13 and 13:3, in first-person form: "Then the word of the LORD came to me a second time, saying . . ." (cf. also Jer. 33:1). In the case of Jeremiah, however, the "second time" means an entirely new question (Jer. 1:13), command (13:3), or promise (33:1). The "second time" here is a repetition of the word that came the first time. Only Jonah among the biblical prophets has to have his assignment given to him twice!

A disobedient prophet could meet with immediate calamity, as is evident in the account about the prophet who disobeyed the Lord's word and was killed by a lion (1 Kings 13:20-32). But here, in an illustration of what Jonah himself will soon declare (4:2), the Lord's compassion and patience allows Jonah a second chance. Though this biblical book has a didactic aim, the Lord does not capitalize on this occasion as a teaching opportunity, declaring, "See there, Jonah! You can't run away from me!" Nor are there heavenly observations on Jonah's foolishness or disobedience. The Lord simply repeats the original assignment.

[2] The word translated "proclamation" ($q^e r\bar{i}'\bar{a}h$) occurs only here in the Hebrew Bible and is a cognate with the verb "proclaim" ($q\bar{a}r\bar{a}'$).[116] The Greek Old Testament translates as *kērygma,* the word used for the apostolic preaching in the New Testament (Rom. 16:25; 1 Cor. 1:21; 15:14; Titus 1:3; "preaching, what we preach" in RSV; "proclamation" in NRSV).[117]

---

[116] The author likes cognate accusatives; see p. 54 n. 54.

[117] *Kērygma* occurs elsewhere in the Greek Old Testament only in 2 Chron. 30:5. The use of the word here is instructive in understanding *kerygma* in the New Testament: "The preaching of Jonah was followed by the repentance of the Ninevites. . . . Christian preaching does not persuade the hearers by beautiful or clever words—otherwise it would only be a matter of words. Preaching does more. It takes place in the spirit and in power. It is thus efficacious" (*TDNT,* 3:715-716).

Jonah 3:1-3a

The closest parallel is in Jer. 19:2: "and proclaim there the words that I
tell you."

Nineveh is once again identified as a "great city." This time nothing is
said about the city's wickedness (1:2); there is no need to harp on that theme.
We are to assume that the Lord's word to Jonah continues with the content of the proclamation "that I am telling you." The narrator does not
indicate the content of the proclamation until 3:4.

[3a] In 1:2-3 the command/fulfillment pattern was broken. This time
the command to "get up . . . go . . . do" is carried out, "So Jonah got up
and went." As in the first scene, Jonah's action is put in theological perspective. A few days earlier, he had sought to run away "from the presence
of the LORD" (1:3 twice). Now his actions are "according to the word of
the LORD," as is proper for a prophet (1 Kings 17:8-10). This expression
is used frequently in connection with prophets in the Deuteronomic History:
of Elijah (2 Kings 1:17; 9:26; 10:17), Elisha (2 Kings 4:44; 7:16), a man
of God (2 Kings 23:16), "his servants the prophets" (2 Kings 24:2). Though
Jonah is never named "prophet" in this book, both "son of Amittai" in
1:1 and "according to the word of the LORD" identify him with the Jonah
of 2 Kings 14:25.

As one reflects on the theological significance of this short scene, the
Lord's patience immediately comes to mind. Without exhortations, without
carping or harping, the Lord reissues the charge that was given to Jonah
in the first place. This act of reassigning without accompanying critical
commentary is an illustration of the characteristics of the Lord soon to
be stated in 4:2.

Second, behind this reassignment is the Lord's urgent concern for the
people of the non-Israelite world, in this case the people of Nineveh. That
which initiates and animates the Jonah story is the assignment in Nineveh
(1:1-3). Here that assignment is repeated, and the first part ("go") is carried
out. The repeating of this assignment, unique among prophetic commis-
sionings, hammers the point home: God cares about the peoples of the
world, be they Ethiopians, Philistines (Amos 9:7), Egyptians—or Assyrians
(Isa. 19:23-24).

Hans Walter Wolff has written about Nineveh:

Nineveh—the name always has a powerful impact as a world city. Just
as the New Testament links Bethlehem and Caesar Augustus, Golgotha
and Pontius Pilate, Paul and Rome, Jesus and all the kingdoms of this
world, so Jonah is linked with Nineveh. To go to Nineveh—that means
for us today: to let the great needs and the great instances of evil in
the world completely determine the direction of our efforts and our life-
work. The message about Christ becomes privatized and diminished if
we don't pay attention to what is going on in Moscow and Washington,

in Asia and Africa, in Berlin and Bonn. Or if we don't see our human failure to care for the sick and the old, our failure in the work of education at home and in the developing countries abroad. Or the monstrous dangers that are connected with manipulating human beings through drugs, and the lack of genuine care of souls. But Jonah is not supposed to go to the whole world. "Go to Nineveh!" Go to the one place whose great needs God has opened your eyes to see. Risk your life and prepare yourself to do that which the Lord commands. Jonah is, after all, an individual.[118]

The artist Marc Chagall did a series of six sketches illustrating the Jonah story.[119] One shows the ship in the storm with Jonah descending into the depths. Another pictures Jonah inside the fish, happily enjoying the ride. Yet another has the fish spewing Jonah out. The series does not end, as is often the case with such illustrations of the Jonah story, with Jonah reclining under the shelter of the specially prepared bush. Chagall's final sketch illustrates 3:3, showing the prophet, staff in hand, body in motion, setting out toward Nineveh. Directly overhead we see the sun — or is it God? — smiling.

The City
3:3b–10

Now the spotlight is on Nineveh. Seven times the city is named in the two scenes of Jonah 3 (vs. 2, 3 twice, 4, 5, 6, 7). To open scene V, the narrator pulls the name of the city around in front of the verb to emphasize it: "now as for Nineveh."[120]

This scene reports Jonah's words in the city (3:3b–4), the reactions of the people (v. 5) and their king (vs. 6–9), and finally the response of God (v. 10).

3b Now as for Nineveh, it was a great city even in God's sight, a three days' walk across. 4 And Jonah started to go through the city, walking for one day; and he proclaimed, "Yet forty days and Nineveh will be overthrown!"[121]

[3b] The narrator communicates the vast size of the city in two ways. First, Nineveh is described as "a great city even in God's sight." The Hebrew

---

[118] *Studien,* 92 (my translation).

[119] See M. Chagall, *Dessins pour la Bible, Verve* 38 (1960), no. 90. Three of these appear in *Bible Review* 6 (August 1990): 28–29. See also the comments of Steffen, *Mysterium,* 139–140.

[120] For further examples of this kind of emphasis, see note 30 on 1:4.

[121] Some critics have thought it advisable to transpose 4:5 to this place (see *BHS*), but such a transposition is not necessary; see the discussion of Sasson, 287ff.

is literally, "great to/for God." The superlative in Hebrew may be expressed by bringing a word into relationship with God.[122] Second, the city is so large that it is "a three days' walk across"; literally, "walking three days." The meaning is that it would take three days to walk across the city, as the next verse makes clear when Jonah walks into it for only one day.

Excavations indicate that Nineveh in the eighth century B.C. was a walled city, trapezoidal in shape, with a total perimeter of about seven and one half miles.[123] The longest distance across the city was about two and three quarters miles. Does this statement mean that Jonah wandered to and fro through the city?[124] Or does it include a day for coming in from the suburbs and a day for returning?[125] Or is it a storyteller's exaggeration, for effect? That which the narrator is communicating is the enormity of the city of Nineveh. As Wolff puts it, "The reader is not supposed to do arithmetic. He is supposed to be lost in astonishment."[126]

At the time the book of Jonah was written, Nineveh had been long destroyed. Named at the beginning and the end of the book and mentioned seven times in this chapter, Nineveh functions as a symbol for the great cities of the world.

A mural on the wall of Siegfrieds Mechanisches Musikkabinett in Rüdesheim, Germany, tells the story of Jonah with the familiar scenes: one sees the great fish, the ship, Jonah sitting and looking over the city. What is striking, however, is that the skyline of Nineveh in the background is in actuality the skyline of nearby Mainz! "Nineveh," says this mural, "is the city nearby that needs to hear the prophetic word."

Since this scene is set in Assyria where the people do not know anything about the Lord (Yahweh), the God of the Hebrews, the more general term *Elohim* is used for God. The city of Nineveh is great "in God's [*Elohim's*] sight" (3:3), the people believe in *Elohim* (3:5) and cry to *Elohim* (3:8).

---

[122] The NRSV translates, "an exceedingly large city." It would appear, however, that in many instances the name of God is used to indicate the superlative by bringing the person or thing into relationship with God; cf. JPS footnote, "a large city of God," and the translation in the current edition of Luther's German Bible, "eine grosse Stadt vor Gott." See Gen. 23:6; 1 Sam. 14:15; Pss. 36:6 [7]; 80:10 [11]; and D. Winton Thomas, "Unusual Ways of Expressing the Superlative in Hebrew," *VT* 3 (1953): 209–224, esp. 215–216.

[123] See pp. 40–42 above.

[124] This was Luther's suggestion: "I understand these words to mean that Nineveh was so large that one needed three days to traverse all its streets, not chasing, but with a leisurely gait such as one usually adopts when strolling on a street. . . . Such a walk does not imply a beeline course, but a walk hither and yon, here and there. However, everyone may adopt whatever view he will" (*Jonah,* 84).

[125] So Wiseman, "Nineveh," *The Illustrated Bible Dictionary,* 2:1090; and idem, "Jonah's Nineveh," *Tyndale Bulletin* 30 (1979): 38.

[126] Wolff, *Obadiah and Jonah,* 148.

The king of Nineveh hopes that *Elohim* will change his mind (3:9), and *Elohim* does so (3:10 twice).[127]

[4] Jonah goes a third of the way into the city, where he delivers his message. Again, the narrator likes to play upon a word. The word translated "proclaim" is the Hebrew verb *qārā'*. It has already occurred several times in the story, requiring a variety of translations: told by the Lord to "preach" against Nineveh, Jonah originally chose to run away (1:1-3). Jonah was told by the captain to "call on" his God, but we do not hear how Jonah responded (1:6). The sailors "cried out" to Yahweh in prayer (1:14) and Jonah eventually "called" to the Lord from the depths of his imprisonment in the great fish (2:2 [3]). Now, finally, he "proclaimed" his message to the people of Nineveh, as he had been told to do in the first place.

Jonah's speech is marked by remarkable brevity and a decided lack of rhetorical creativity. Contrary to the usual prophetic practice in announcing judgment, the destruction of the city is merely announced, with no reason provided.[128]

What language did the prophet speak as he delivered his prophetic message in Nineveh? Was it Aramaic, the international language of diplomacy of the day (Isa. 36:11)? Or did he use a translator (Gen. 42:23)? The story does not concern itself with such details. Rudolph suggests: "The God who confused human languages (Genesis 11) could also see to it that those who spoke different languages understood one another (Acts 2)."[129]

"Forty days" is a favorite biblical period of time. It designates the length of the flood (Gen. 7:4, 12, 17), the time Moses spent on Mount Sinai (Ex. 24:18; 34:28; Deut. 9:9, 11, 18, 25), the time for the mission of the spies (Num. 13:25; cf. 14:34), the duration of Goliath's taunting (1 Sam. 17:16), the time of Elijah's journey to Horeb/Sinai (1 Kings 19:8) as well as the time of Jesus' fasting (Matt. 4:2; Mark 1:13; Luke 4:2). Jonah's short speech has a biblical ring![130]

The biblical ring continues with the announcement that Nineveh will be "overthrown." This is the word used in connection with the account of the destruction of the cities of Sodom and Gomorrah (Gen. 19:21, 25, 29). Because of their depravity, the cities were destroyed by an act of God and left as a pile of smoking rubble (Gen. 19:28). The destruction of these cities was remembered by the biblical writers as an especially dramatic instance of God's punishment (again, with the same word "overthrow":

---

[127] See Excursus, "The Names for God in Jonah," pp. 45-46.

[128] Contrast, e.g., the accusation/announcement of punishment pattern in Amos 1:3-5, 6-8, etc.; 4:1-3; 8:4-8; Isa. 1:21-26; 3:16-4:1.

[129] Rudolph, 356 (my translation).

[130] The Greek translations have "three days" here, which has no basis in the Hebrew and must have been picked up from 3:3.

Deut. 29:23; Isa. 13:19; Jer. 20:16; 49:18; 50:40; Lam. 4:6; Amos 4:11).
Those hearing this word used in connection with the coming punishment
of Nineveh would be reminded of the stories of Sodom and Gomorrah.
   The book of Tobit, written in the second century B.C., remembers
Jonah's short announcement of Nineveh's doom. The aged Tobit, living
in Nineveh, speaks to his son and grandchildren from his deathbed. He
advises them to leave Nineveh:

> Go to Media, my son, for I fully believe what Jonah the prophet said
> about Nineveh, that it will be overthrown. . . . So now, my son, leave
> Nineveh, because what the prophet Jonah said will surely happen. (Tobit
> 14:4, 8, RSV)[131] [132]

Jonah's speech is only five words in Hebrew: "Yet forty days and-
Nineveh shall-be-overthrown!" Hearers familiar with Hebrew traditions
would perhaps recognize in this 3 + 2 pattern the rhythm of the *qinah,* or
lament (cf. Amos 5:2; Lam. 1:3a; 2:4a; etc.).

**5 Then the people of Nineveh believed in God; and they proclaimed
a fast and they put on mourning garments, from the greatest to the least
of them.   6 And word reached the king of Nineveh, and he got up from
his throne and took off his robe, covered himself with sackcloth and
sat in ashes.   7 Then he had a proclamation made in Nineveh: "By the
decree of the king and his nobles: No human being and no animal, no
herd or flock, shall taste anything. They shall not eat food and they
shall not drink water.   8 And human beings and animals shall be
covered with sackcloth and they shall cry mightily to God. And all shall
turn from their evil ways and from the violence that is in their hands.
9 Who knows? God may turn and change his mind and turn from the
heat of his anger and we will not die."**

[5]   As was the case with the non-Israelite sailors (1:16), so now, given
just a glimpse of the reality of the true God by one of God's prophets,
the citizens of Nineveh immediately believe! Deeply convicted of their sin-
fulness, they call a fast and put on sackcloth.
   Fasting in the Old Testament could apply either to an individual or to
the whole community. When David's child became deathly ill, the king
wept and fasted for a week (2 Sam. 12:16). Ancient Israel "proclaimed

---

[131] This RSV text is based on Codices Vaticanus, Alexandrinus, and Venetus as well
as other manuscripts; Sinaiticus, the Old Latin, and the Syrian translation do not mention
Jonah here (see NRSV and *Tobit,* ed. R. Hanhart [Göttingen: Vandenhoeck & Ruprecht,
1983]).
[132] In an Islamic retelling of the Jonah story from around A.D. 1200, Jonah's speech in
Nineveh sounds very much like the central creed of Islam: "There is no God but God, and
Mohammed is his prophet" (*Tales of the Prophets of al-Kisa'i;* see Appendix, p. 115).

a fast" when facing a dire military threat (Jer. 36:9; 2 Chron. 20:3), when God's guidance for the community was especially needed (Ezra 8:21), or in connection with a legal procedure (1 Kings 21:9, 12). A natural disaster, such as a grasshopper plague, could occasion the calling of a fast (Joel 1:14; 2:15). A fast was an intergenerational event for the whole community, including the children (2 Chron. 20:13; Joel 2:16; Jonah 3:5) and even the animals (Jonah 3:7–8; Judith 4:9–11). Actions associated with the fast demonstrated or brought about humility by taking away beauty. Those fasting wore sackcloth, put dirt on their heads, and sat in ashes (Jonah 3:6–9; Jer. 4:8; Neh. 9:1). Since fasts were occasioned by national emergencies, fast days were proclaimed as needed; in a later period, there were also set times for fasting (Zech. 7:3, 5; 8:19). Postexilic prophecy delivered a critique of a kind of fasting that was not coupled with social justice and love for the hungry and poor (Isa. 58:3–9[133]).

"From the greatest to the least" indicates that everyone in Nineveh takes part in the fast. Naming the extremes indicates the inclusion of the whole group (merismus).[134]

[6] The story of Jonah testifies to the power of the word (Heb. root, *dbr*) of God and to the reaction it brings about. Once again, the author plays upon a Hebrew root: The "word (*dbr*) of the LORD" came to Jonah, telling him to go to Nineveh and "preach against it." A second time the "word (*dbr*) of the LORD" came to Jonah (3:1), telling him to go to Nineveh and "proclaim against it the proclamation that I am telling (*dbr*) you." This time Jonah went to Nineveh "according to the word (*dbr*) of the LORD." And this time the content of that word is given: "Yet forty days and Nineveh will be overthrown" (3:4).

Jonah's "word" — the saying about the overthrow of Nineveh — "reached the king," and the king responded: "he got up . . . and took off . . . covered himself . . . and sat" (3:6). Later we discover that the Lord saw the reaction of the king and people of Nineveh and the Lord called off the evil that he said (*dbr*) he would do to them. The word to be fulfilled in "yet forty days" is rescinded and the Lord does not "do" it (3:10). Once a word from the Lord has been spoken, it stands "out there," having a "quasi-objective existence until it enters into the event that is its fulfillment"; see Isa. 55:10–11.[135]

The reactions of the king upon hearing the word about the coming overthrow of Nineveh are immediate and, for the hearers of this story,

---

[133] Along with Jonah, this is one of the assigned texts for the observance of Yom Kippur in Judaism.

[134] For other examples of merismus in Jonah, see p. 27 above. Other examples of large-small merismus: 1 Sam. 20:2; Esth. 1:5, 20; 2 Chron. 31:15; 34:30; 36:18; see Vanoni, 85.

[135] I owe this formulation to Prof. John V. Halvorson.

exemplary: "and he got up . . . and took off . . . covered . . . and sat."[136]
Once again, the people of the world are demonstrating to the people of
God how they ought to conduct themselves! The behavior of these Ninevites
stands in sharp contrast, for example, to the response of King Jehoiakim
of Judah and his cronies to the word of the Lord as brought by Jeremiah
(Jer. 36:3, 20–25).[137] The actions of the Ninevites would long stand as a
model response to prophetic preaching (Matt. 12:41; Luke 11:32). The narrator engages in a play on words: the king leaves his throne (root, *kissē'*)
and puts on (root, *kissāh*) sackcloth and sits in ashes. These actions express
humility in the face of coming disaster (Jer. 6:26; Esth. 4:1–3) or con-
trition with the hope of calling forth help from God (Neh. 9:1; Dan. 9:3;
Judith 4:8–15).

[7] The word *ṭa'am,* "decree," is used as a noun with this sense only
here in the Hebrew part of the Old Testament; the Aramaic cognate *ṭe'ēm*
occurs often with the sense of a decree from a king.[138] The broad categories
"no human being and no animal" (*'ādām* and *behēmāh*) denote humans
and all the creatures on earth (Ex. 9:25; 12:12; Ps. 135:8; Jer. 21:6; 27:5;
etc.).[139] "Herd or flock" refers to cattle and sheep, frequently mentioned
together (Gen. 13:5; 20:14; 21:27; 24:35; Deut. 8:13). The verb "taste" is
ṭa'am, from the same root as the noun meaning "decree." Again, the author
is playing on words. The meaning is to sample a small quantity; cf. 1 Sam.
14:24, 29, 43; 2 Sam. 3:35.

[8]   When Jerusalem was threatened by the Assyrians, King Hezekiah
and his cabinet officers and the senior priests all covered themselves with
sackcloth as a gesture of humility, then presented themselves to Isaiah the
prophet, asking for his prayers for the nation (2 Kings 19:1–2; cf. also
2 Sam. 3:31; Joel 1:13). In Nineveh, both humans and animals are "covered
with sackcloth."

This is one of many biblical illustrations of the solidarity between
humans and animals. At the time of the grasshopper plague reported in
the book of Joel, the animals (*behēmāh*) groan and even cry out to the
Lord (Joel 1:18, 20). The animals of the field, and even the land itself,
can be told to "fear not" (Joel 2:21–22) because of what the Lord will do.
Since both humans and animals are creatures of the sixth day (Gen. 1:24–25;
here *behēmāh* is translated "cattle"), the relationship between them is close.
Even wild animals may be described as serving a king (Jer. 27:6). Humans,
the animals, and the land are all viewed as God's creation. The book of

---

[136] Cf. also the anticipated reactions of the princes of surrounding nations at the fall
of Tyre, Ezek. 26:15–18.

[137] See Wolff, *Obadiah and Jonah,* 145–146.

[138] For a listing, see p. 29 above.

[139] On the merismus here, see p. 27 above.

Judith reports that when the people of Jerusalem were threatened by the Assyrian army:

> Every man of Israel cried to God with great fervor, and they humbled themselves with much fasting. They and their wives and their children and their cattle and every resident alien and hired laborer and purchased slave—they all put sackcloth around their waists. (Judith 4:9–10)

As in Jonah, there is a solidarity between human beings and the animals, with all joining in these rites of humility before the Lord. Other texts indicate that the Lord hears the cry of the hungry ravens (Ps. 147:9; Job 38:41; Luke 12:24) and provides food for all creatures, human and animal alike (Pss. 104:27–30; 145:15–16). The book of Jonah closes with a declaration of God's concern for the animals (4:11).

When the king calls upon his subjects to "turn from their evil ways" he is using the language of the Hebrew prophets (Jer. 15:7; 18:11; 23:22; 25:5; 26:3; 35:15; 36:3, 7; Ezek. 3:19; 13:22; 18:23; 20:44, 33:9, 11; Zech. 1:4) as well as that of the Deuteronomic historian (1 Kings 13:33; 2 Kings 17:13) and the wisdom teachers (Prov. 2:12; 8:13; 28:10; cf. 2 Chron. 7:14). The prophets criticized the Assyrians for their arrogance and brutality in international affairs (Isa. 10:12–19; Nahum 3). The author of Jonah, however, is shaping the Assyrian king according to the model of Israelite piety. "Their evil ways" refers to paths that are traveled by the feet; the king also asks that the people turn away from the "violence" that their hands do (cf. 1 Chron. 12:17; Job 16:17; for hands and feet, Isa. 59:6–8). "Violence" can refer to extremely wild and ruthless acts, such as the murder of seventy men at one place (Judg. 9:24; cf. v. 5), and often refers specifically to urban crime (Ps. 55:9; Jer. 6:7; Ezek. 7:23; Micah 6:12).

[9] The king asks, "Who knows?" Similar constructions occur in two other biblical contexts: (1) The child of David and Bathsheba died after a week's illness. While the child was ill, David neither ate nor drank, spending the time in fasting and weeping. After the child died, David took up his normal activities, explaining that he fasted while the child was still alive because he thought, "Who knows? The LORD may be gracious to me, and the child may live" (2 Sam. 12:22). (2) The book of Joel tells the story of a terrible locust plague. In the midst of the plague, the prophet urges the people, "Return to the LORD. . . . Who knows whether he will not turn and relent, and leave a blessing behind him . . . ?" (Joel 2:13–14).

The situation is the same in Jonah. In each of these three cases, the "Who knows?" is spoken during a fast. In the first example, David was fasting for an individual; in the second, all the people were fasting for the sake of the community; in the case of Jonah, an entire non-Israelite community is fasting. Even David, the "man after God's own heart," did not pretend to control God. There was no guarantee that fasting would bring about the desired response on God's part. In the case of David, it did not. Nor did the prophet Joel claim to control God's actions. The king of Nineveh, a non-Israelite, follows in this exemplary tradition. He knows that fasting carries no guarantee that God will save him and his people, but, on the other hand, "Who knows?" Note also the attitude of King Jehoshaphat when Judah faced a military crisis. He called a national fast, prayed, and then left things in the hands of God: "We do not know what to do, but our eyes are upon thee" (2 Chron. 20:12).

The Hebrew behind "change . . . mind" is the verb *niham*. In the *niphal* conjugation, as here, it can mean to be sorry, to rue, to repent, to change one's mind.[140] The verb occurs some thirty-three times in the *niphal*. In four of these occurrences (Ex. 13:17; Job 42:6; Jer. 8:6; 31:19) it has a human subject. For example, Exodus 13 reports that God did not lead the Israelites through Philistine territory, because God thought, "If the people face war, they may change their minds and return to Egypt" (Ex. 13:17). The sense here is to change one's mind in a way that leads to a reversal of action.

The remaining twenty-nine occurrences have God or Yahweh as subject and may be categorized as follows:

1. The verb may report the Lord's past actions. The Lord was "sorry" for making humans (Gen. 6:6, 7), for making Saul king (1 Sam. 15:11, 35), or for the evil done to the people (Jer. 42:10[141]). The verb may also refer to the fact that disasters came upon the people without the Lord having "pity" or "relenting" (Jer. 20:16; Zech. 8:14).

2. The verb may refer to the Lord's future actions, most often calling off an announced punishment (Amos 7:3, 6; Jer. 18:8; 26:3, 13, 19; Ex. 32:12, 14; 2 Sam. 24:16 = 1 Chron. 21:15; cf. the negatives Ezek. 24:14; Jer. 4:28; 1 Sam. 15:29 twice). The basis for calling off the punishment is the Lord's steadfast love (Ps. 106:45).

In Jer. 18:10, however, it is stated that the Lord will change his mind about doing some future good. Psalm 110:4 states that the Lord will not change his mind in regard to the appointment of the priest-king.

3. In two instances, the verb occurs in a creedlike statement describing Yahweh, who is:

> gracious and merciful,
> slow to anger and abounding in steadfast love,
> and changes his mind about punishing.
>   (Joel 2:13, my translation)

---

[140] On this theme, see Jörg Jeremias, *Die Reue Gottes,* esp. 98–113.
[141] But cf. the comments of Jeremias, *Die Reue,* 81–82.

Or Jonah addresses God as:

> gracious and merciful,
> slow to anger, and abounding in steadfast love,
> and changing your mind about punishing.
>
> (Jonah 4:2, my translation)

Will the Lord always have mercy and call off an announced punishment, if the people are genuinely sorry and repent? No one can presume to answer that question. The prophet Joel says, "Who knows?" (Joel 2:14).

Here the king of Nineveh is hoping that if the people of Nineveh sincerely repent, the Lord will change his mind about the punishment Jonah has announced. Of course the Assyrian king as portrayed here would not know the sort of creedal statements used by Joel and in Jonah 4:2. Nor would he know the long tradition of the Lord changing his mind and calling off evil. The king can't be sure, but like the sea captain quoted in 1:6, he can hope that God will act "and we will not die." He is kindred to another Gentile, a centurion, who also did not presume upon the Lord's help, and of whom Jesus said, "I tell you, not even in Israel have I found such faith" (Luke 7:1-10). The king does not presume to dictate to God, nor does he assume that God will automatically react favorably to his penitence and that of his people (and the animals). He only expresses a hopeful "Who knows?"[142]

10 And God saw what they did, how they turned from their evil ways; and God changed his mind about the evil which he said he would do against them, and he did not do it.

[10] Once again, when these citizens of non-Israelite Nineveh are meant, the more general term "God" (*Elohim*) is used.[143] The king's proclamation had decreed that the people of Nineveh should "turn from their evil ways and from the violence that is in their hands" (3:8). Here it is reported that God saw them doing just that.

The evil that God said he would bring upon them had been succinctly announced in Jonah's short proclamation (3:4b). Now the announced punishment has been called off. This narrative exemplifies that which will

---

[142] The Targum on Jonah (first century A.D.) became one of the standard texts for the observance of Yom Kippur, a day for repentance and the announcement of forgiveness of sins. Those who produced the Targum were not happy with the uncertainty about what God would do as expressed here and therefore changed this verse: "Whoever knows that there are sins on his conscience let him repent of them and we will be pitied before the Lord, and he will turn back from the vehemence of his anger, and we will not perish" (Cathcart and Gordon, 108). See also the comments of Levine, 88-89.

[143] See Excursus, "The Names for God in Jonah," pp. 45-46 above.

be said in the form of a confession of faith in God in 4:2 (changing your mind about punishing).

When those in the postexilic Jewish community heard this book read, they would have remembered that this sort of thing had happened before. Moses had interceded for the people after the regrettable incident with the golden calf. He had prayed, "Turn from your fierce wrath; change your mind and do not bring disaster on your people," and the Lord changed his mind (Ex. 32:12-14). The postexilic audience would also recall what had happened in connection with another prophet, like Jonah, a contemporary of Jeroboam. The Lord had twice called off an announced—or illustrated—punishment after Amos had interceded for them (Amos 7:3, 6). The story here provides an example of what Jeremiah had learned from the Lord at the potter's house (Jer. 18:8) and of what he had tried to communicate to the people of Jerusalem (Jer. 26:3, 13, 19).

Thus God changing his mind about punishing was not without precedent. Two things are especially noteworthy about God's change of mind in the Jonah story, however. First, the punishment was to have been directed not against God's people but against Nineveh. That which Israel knew and confessed about God's love and patience toward themselves (4:2) apparently was also true about God's relationship to the other people of the world! Second, in the other examples given, the people had an advocate with God. Moses appealed to public opinion and to historical promises in arguing with the Lord on the people's behalf. Amos pleaded with God for Israel's sake. Jeremiah's temple sermon urged the people to amend their ways. Jonah, however, had no interest in taking up the Assyrian cause. The next scene will make that quite clear.

In summarizing what scene V has to teach about God, we begin with two observations about the scene as a whole. First, this is the only instance in which the Bible portrays a prophet walking down the streets of one of the great non-Israelite cities of the world. Jonah is not in Jerusalem, nor even in Bethel or Samaria, but in the Assyrian capital. The reader of the New Testament is reminded of Paul walking the streets of the great world city of his day, Athens (Acts 17:15-34). Second, this is the only scene in the story where the name Yahweh, translated "the Lord," does not appear. This second observation is related to the first. Just as Paul accommodated himself to the theological understanding of those in Athens, respecting the spirit behind whoever constructed the altar "to an unknown god" (Acts 17:23), so the author of Jonah now consistently speaks of Elohim, translated "God," in describing the prophet's work in this city (Jonah 3:5, 8, 9, 10). The scene is a refreshingly secular one, with nothing of the sacrifices and songs of the sanctuary, nothing of traditional theological jargon (Jonah's sermon is a complete success in using nontheological vocabulary!), only a lone prophet walking the streets of a strange city as Paul would one day walk the streets of Athens.

In the first part of the scene, the prophet announces that God's doomsday clock is ticking (3:3b–4). Like one nation delivering a time-conditioned ultimatum to another ("withdraw from that territory by the fifteenth of next month"), Jonah's word announces that destruction will come, but not for a number of days. The people have been warned. Theologically considered, there is behind the "yet forty days" a glimmer of God's patience and love.

The second part of this scene reports the total and exemplary nature of the response of the people, the king, even the animals (3:5–9). They not only "turn around," reorienting their lives, but they "turn away from" their previous corrupt practices.[144]

The holiest day in the Jewish calendar is Yom Kippur, the Day of Atonement. Since around A.D. 200, the afternoon reading for Yom Kippur has been the story of Jonah,[145] paired with Isaiah 58, which speaks about the nature of true fasting (Isa. 58:4–7). Year after year, in synagogues throughout the world, the people of the non-Israelite city of Nineveh are held up as examples of a proper attitude of repentance. The *Pirke de Rabbi Eliezer* gives an imaginative interpretation of the fasting here described:

> The men were on one side, and the women on the other, and their children were by themselves; all the clean animals were on one side, and their offspring were by themselves. The infants saw the breasts of their mothers, (and they wished) to have suck, and they wept. The mothers saw their children, (and they wished) to give them suck. By the merit of 4123 children more than twelve hundred thousand men (were saved).[146]

An illustration for the book of Jonah in *The Duke of Alba's Castillian Bible,* a joint Jewish-Catholic project of A.D. 1430, portrays the scene described by Eliezer: we see the lambs, the goats, the children, all being kept away from their mothers.[147]

The response of the citizens of this city has been held up as exemplary not only in Judaism. Jesus commended them, "because they repented at the proclamation of Jonah" (Matt. 12:41; Luke 11:32). The Midrash on

---

[144] "More clearly than in the book of Joel, 'conversion' is here understood as 'turning away from' wrong behavior" (Jeremias, *Die Reue,* 106, my translation).

[145] "On the Day of Atonement we read . . . and for *haftarah* the book of Jonah" (*Megillah* 31a, *The Babylonian Talmud* [London: Soncino Press, 1938], 188).

[146] *PRE,* 343. See Appendix 3.1 (pp. 104–108).

[147] Carl-Otto Nordstrom, *The Duke of Alba's Castillian Bible* (Uppsala: Almqvist & Wiksell, 1967), 192–196.

Jonah gives a number of concrete illustrations of Nineveh's repentance.[148] The Koran also holds up the Ninevites as exemplary because of their faith.[149]

Yet another commendable aspect of the people of this world city is the attitude of the king, expressed in the "Who knows?" of his own proclamation. Here is no assumption of automatic forgiveness. This non-Hebrew monarch takes his place alongside the monarchs and prophets in Israel who expressed the same attitude (2 Sam. 12:22; Joel 2:14).

The scene concludes with the announcement of God's change of plans (3:10). This dramatic change illustrates the theological instruction Jeremiah had received in the pottery shop:

> Can I not do with you, O house of Israel, just as this potter has done? says the LORD. Just like the clay in the potter's hand, so are you in my hand. . . . At one moment I may declare concerning a nation or a kingdom, that I will pluck up and break down and destroy it, but if that nation, concerning which I have spoken, turns from its evil, I will change my mind about the disaster that I intended to bring on it. (Jer. 18:6-8)

When citizens take seriously a word from God and turn the life of their city around, it is possible that God may change plans and call off an announced punishment. God had done it before (Ex. 32:11-14; Amos 7:1-3). Jonah had been afraid all along that God might do it again (4:2).

The Confession
4:1-3

One of the issues driving the story of Jonah from the beginning has been: What will happen to the city of Nineveh, whose wickedness is so great that it has come to the attention of the Lord? That issue has now been resolved. The people of Nineveh heard the prophetic word, they reordered their lives, and the announced destruction has been called off.

Another issue remains. What will happen to a prophet who disobeys the Lord? Jonah has discovered that it is impossible to run away from the Lord. His preaching in Nineveh, it would seem, has been marvelously successful. One would think he would be overjoyed. But as this scene opens, Jonah is angry.

A brief narrative introduction reporting Jonah's anger sets the scene (4:1). Jonah explains why he ran away and recites a creed in traditional

---

[148] See Appendix 3.3 (pp. 109-113).
[149] See Appendix 4.1 (pp. 113-115).

biblical language (4:2). The story takes a shocking turn when Jonah expresses a wish to die (4:3). The Masoretic text calls for a pause at this point in the story, inserting a *setumah,* an indicator for a major break, in the text.[150]

4:1 But Jonah was absolutely furious[151] and burned with anger. 2 So he prayed to the LORD and said, "O please, LORD, was this not what I said when I was still in my own country? That is why I ran away to Tarshish in the first place, because I knew that you are a God who is compassionate and merciful, slow to anger and filled with steadfast love and ready to change your mind about punishing. 3 So now, Lord, please take my life from me, for it is better for me to die than to live."

[4:1] Once again the author is playing upon a few favorite words. The previous chapter spoke of the people of Nineveh turning from their *evil* (*rā'āh*) ways (3:8). God saw that they had turned from their *evil* (*rā'āh*) ways (3:10) and therefore changed his mind about bringing evil (*rā'āh*) upon them (3:10).

And now, what about Jonah? These events have caused him to be "absolutely furious" (*rā'āh*); the word is the same as that translated "evil" in the previous chapter. God has turned from his fury while Jonah is absolutely furious; God has turned from the "heat [root, *ḥrh*] of his anger" (3:9) while Jonah is burning up (root, *ḥrh*) with it. Several times this chapter speaks of Jonah's burning anger: he is also angry at the rescue of Nineveh (4:4) and at the death of the plant that provided shade (4:9 twice).[152]

[2] Just as Jonah had "prayed" to the Lord from the fish (1:17 [2:1]; the Hebrew verbs are identical), now he prays again. The prayer begins with a respectful "O please, LORD." Even with such a respectful beginning Jonah is only imitating the prayer of the non-Israelite sailors (1:14). "Was this not what I said . . . ?" occurs only here and in Ex. 14:12. Does the author of Jonah have Exodus 14 in mind?[153]

Jonah says, "That is why I ran away," now making clear why he tried to avoid going to Nineveh in the first place. While he was still in his home country of Israel and was given the Nineveh assignment, he had suspected that the people of that city might repent. Because he knew something about

---

[150] The Dead Sea text also indicates a break here, leaving an empty line after v. 3; *Les grottes de Murabba'ât,* ed. Benoît, Milik, and de Vaux, DJD, 2:191.

[151] Lit., "displeased with great displeasure." Once again the cognate accusative construction is used to express emphasis (see note 54 on 1:10); note the contrasting cognate accusative in 4:6.

[152] Cf. the anger of Cain and the Lord's question about it (Gen. 4:5-6). Cain, too, ran away "from the presence of the LORD" (Gen. 4:16; cf. Jonah 1:3, 3, 10). Is the Jonah story drawing upon these reminiscences from Genesis 4? See Vanoni, 143.

[153] Cf. also Jonah 1:16 and Ex. 14:31; see note 35 on 1:5.

the nature of the Lord who gave him the assignment, he also suspected that if they did repent, the Lord might call off the punishment. Jonah did not want the people of Nineveh to repent and be forgiven, which is why he tried to run away to Tarshish. Three times the narrator has described Jonah's flight as being "from before the presence of YHWH" (1:3 twice, 10). Now when Jonah himself talks about his flight, he admits no rebelling against the Lord. He speaks only of running away to Tarshish (4:2).[154]

Jonah says, "I knew that you are a God who is compassionate and merciful, slow to anger and filled with steadfast love and ready to change your mind about punishing." As the story has already demonstrated (1:9; 2:2–9), Jonah once again indicates that he is well acquainted with the religious tradition in which he stands. His prayer is steeped in typical biblical language, as the following table indicates:[155]

	compassionate/ gracious	merciful	slow to anger	abounding in love	changing mind
Jonah 4:2	x	x	x	x	x
Joel 2:13	x	x	x	x	x
Ps. 145:8	x	x	x	x	-
Neh. 9:17	x	x	x	x (great in)	-
Ex. 34:6–7	x (2)	x (1)	x	x	-
Ps. 86:15	x (2)	x (1)	x	x	-
Ps. 103:8	x (2)	x (1)	x	x	-
Ps. 111:4	x	x	-	-	-
2 Chron. 30:9	x	x	-	-	-
Num. 14:18	-	-	x	x	-
Neh. 9:31	x	x	-	-	-

There are five elements in Jonah's prayer, which is a confession of faith. The only other five-element confession in the Old Testament is in Joel 2, where the confession provides the reason for a call to "return to the LORD." In Exodus 34 and in Psalms 86 and 103, the order of the first two elements is "merciful and gracious."

The adjective "compassionate" or "gracious" (*ḥannûn*) occurs thirteen times in the Old Testament and is used only in reference to God.[156] Exodus

---

[154] Magonet, *Form,* 93.

[155] The closest parallel is Joel 2:13. Though the matter of dating and the direction of dependency remains uncertain, it seems more likely that the author of Jonah is picking up quotations from Joel and dividing them (3:9; 4:2) than that Joel is assembling his liturgy from Jonah; Vanoni (p. 140) suggests that if Joel were going to quote, he would be more likely to quote from the great intercession of Moses than from the pagan king of Nineveh! See also Sasson, 282f.

[156] Does Ps. 112:4 refer to God? So RSV; but see the marginal note and NRSV.

22:27 illustrates the meaning of the word: If a person's coat is taken as collateral for a loan, it should be returned before sundown, because it might be needed for warmth. If that person cries to the Lord, the Lord says, "I will hear, because I am compassionate."

The Hebrew for "merciful," *raḥûm,* is related to *reḥem,* the word for womb, and thus has something of the sense of "motherly love." This adjective also occurs thirteen times in the Old Testament, always in reference to God.[157] "Compassionate and merciful" are paired in Jonah 4:2; Joel 2:13; Neh. 9:17, 31; Pss. 111:4; 145:8; 2 Chron. 30:9; in the order "merciful and compassionate": Ex. 34:6; Pss. 86:15; 103:8.

The literal Hebrew for "slow to anger" has the sense "long of anger"; the word is also used to describe an eagle with "long pinions" (Ezek. 17:3). Being "slow to anger" is one of the virtues described in Proverbs; it is the opposite of having a hasty temper (Prov. 14:29) or a hot temper (15:18) and is better than might (16:32) or pride (Eccl. 7:8). The expression is used of the Lord in the passages listed in the table above as well as in Nahum 1:3 and Jer. 15:15 ("forbearance").

In addition to the occurrences listed in the table above, the phrase "abounding in steadfast love" occurs in prayers, such as Neh. 13:22 and Pss. 5:7 [8]; 69:13 [14]; 106:7, 45.[158] "Steadfast love" translates the Hebrew *ḥesed.* We may bring the sense of this word into focus by looking at its usage in a nontheological context. David and Jonathan made a covenant with each other, sealing their friendship (1 Sam. 18:1–3). Later, Jonathan asked David to remember him and his family, no matter what the future might bring, saying, "If I am still alive, show me the loyal love (*ḥesed*) of the LORD . . . and do not cut off your loyalty (*ḥesed*) from my house for ever" (1 Sam. 20:14–15). Thus the meaning of the word is love, with a strong element of loyalty, between two parties who have made a formal pledge to each other through a covenant. It can also be used to describe the loyal love between two parties in a marriage (Jer. 2:2, "devotion," and Hos. 2:19).

The book of the prophet Hosea is especially instructive in understanding the meaning of *ḥesed.* The word may denote God's love for God's people (Hos. 2:19). It may also refer to the people's love to the neighbor (Hos. 4:1, "kindness"). In Hos. 6:4 and 6:6, *ḥesed* refers to the people's loyal love to God, or, more accurately, to their lack of it. In addition, the book of Hosea presents two unforgettable examples of *ḥesed* in family life: though his wife was unfaithful, Hosea continued to love her, forgave her,

---

[157] Unless Ps. 112:4 is an exception; see previous note.

[158] Note the occurrence of *niḥam* in v. 45, translated "showed compassion"; see the comments on 3:9.

and took her back (Hosea 3). Just as a parent continues to love a rebelling child, so the Lord continues to love a rebellious people (Hosea 11). The biblical writers never tire of praising the Lord's loyal love, or *ḥesed,* described as abundant (the examples above), filling the earth (Pss. 33:5; 119:64), and everlasting (Psalm 136, each verse). Jonah knows something of this steadfast love and knows that when God's people cry for help, God will respond because of that steadfast love (Ps. 106:40–45).

The story of Jonah makes clear that this steadfast love is not limited to God's own people. Now it is the Assyrians who have cried mightily to God. God has responded to their cry, too, by calling off the destruction that Jonah had announced.

The story itself has just provided an illustration of what Jonah means when he says to God that "you are . . . ready to change your mind about punishing" (3:10).[159]

[3] The expression "and now" (*weʿattāh*) often draws a practical conclusion from what has been said (Ps. 39:7; Gen. 3:22; Isa. 5:3, 5). Here, after this general statement about the nature of the Lord, the prophet concludes that he would be better off dead.

Jonah prays, "Take my life from me." Elijah once expressed such a death wish. Queen Jezebel had issued an order to kill Elijah because of his involvement in the execution of the Baal prophets on Mount Carmel. Fearing for his life, the prophet went into the wilderness and sat under a broom tree. He prayed in words almost identical to Jonah 4:3: "Now, LORD, take away my life" (1 Kings 19:4). Like Elijah, Jonah asks the Lord to take his life. His reasons, however, are quite different from those of Elijah. Jonah wants to die because he doesn't like the thought of the people of Nineveh being allowed to live. Jonah "has Elijah's despondency . . . without Elijah's excuse."[160] Jeremias observes: "If Elijah wanted to die because of the lack of success of his efforts, Jonah wishes to die because he had more success than he really wanted!"[161] Elijah and Jonah were not the only ones to express death wishes; Moses (Ex. 32:32; Num. 11:15), Job (Job 6:8–9), and Jeremiah (Jer. 20:14–18) did the same. The *Midrash Jonah* suggests that Jonah wants to die because, having lost his clothing and hair in the belly of the fish, he was being made miserable by flies, mosquitoes, ants, and fleas.[162]

To hear anyone express a wish to die is a shocking thing. For a prophet

---

[159] For the notion of God's change of mind, see the comments on 3:9. Jeremias (*Die Reue,* 94) suggests that "the book of Jonah is a unique exposition of this statement."

[160] S. R. Driver, *Introduction to the Literature of the Old Testament* (New York: Charles Scribner's Sons, 1920), 325.

[161] *Die Reue,* 102 (my translation).

[162] For the text, see Appendix, p. 112.

of the Lord to express such a wish is doubly shocking. The Masoretic text has a *setumah* here, indicating that a pause should be made in the reading of the story at this point.[163] The Dead Sea Scroll also indicates a pause here.[164] Following this ancient and traditional structural hint, we break the narrative here. It is effective for the reader or hearer to stop and to ponder Jonah's statement in silence.

In considering the theological significance of this scene we begin with an observation: The action in all but one of the preceding scenes was initiated by the Lord, either with a word (1:1; 3:1; 4:4) or an act (1:4; 1:17). The action in this sixth scene begins with words of Jonah, in fact with words of anger directed to the Lord. The remainder of the chapter is marked by give-and-take, the Lord responding to Jonah with words (4:4), Jonah countering with action (4:5), the Lord acting and Jonah initiating another verbal exchange (4:6–9), and finally the Lord's concluding speech (4:10). If theology is that which is said about God, the theology presented here is not worked out in calm reflection upon the Divine. Rather, it is the result of this passionate interchange between God and Jonah.

The most obvious concentration of statements about God in the book of Jonah is found in Jonah's confession in 4:2. Earlier, Jonah had declared his faith in the Lord, the creator (1:9) and the deliverer (2:6b; cf. 2:2a, 9b). The story illustrates these notions in narrative form: the creator controls the forces of nature (1:4, 15; 4:8) as well as nature's animals and plants (1:17; 2:10; 4:6, 7). The deliverer rescues Jonah from the great fish (2:10). Supplementing what is said about God and nature in 1:9 and about God and people in Jonah 2 is this statement in 4:2. Here are listed the characteristics of the God of Israel, with language deeply rooted in biblical tradition. The narrative itself illustrates each of these: God's compassion and mercy (saving Jonah and sparing Nineveh), patience and steadfast love (patience with Jonah, love toward Nineveh), and readiness to have a change of mind about punishment (the canceling of Nineveh's death sentence).

But the *setumah* suggests only a brief pause for reflection. What more does the story have to tell?

The Question
4:4–11

The Lord initiates the action in this final scene, this time with a question directed to Jonah (4:4). Jonah responds to the question by walking off the set. He takes up a new position to the east of the city where

---

[163] See also 2:9 [10].
[164] See note 150.

he builds a shelter to provide some shade (4:5). Again, the Lord God takes the initiative by "appointing" a plant, a worm, and a wind; Jonah reacts with the expression of yet another death wish (4:6–8). The story concludes with a question-and-answer exchange between God and Jonah (4:9) and then with a thirty-nine-word speech of the Lord, balancing Jonah's thirty-nine-word speech in 4:2 (4:10–11).[165] The end of the story links with the beginning, picking up the theme "Nineveh, that great city" from 1:2, then developing and concretizing it in the picture of 120,000 helpless people, along with a considerable animal population.

The closing question invites Jonah—and each hearer or reader—to become involved by responding with an answer.

4 And the LORD said, "Is it right for you to be so angry?" 5 Then Jonah went out[166] from the city, and sat to the east of the city. He made a booth for himself there, and sat under it in the shade, until he should see what happened to the city.

[4]   The pause in the story has ended. The silence is broken with a word from the Lord. For the first time we listen in on an exchange between the Lord and Jonah. The Lord asks three questions. Jonah responds first with an act, then with a statement. The Lord's final question is left hanging. The theme of Jonah's anger was introduced in 4:1. This is the first of two instances where the Lord asks Jonah whether that anger is appropriate.

[5]   Jonah responds to the Lord's question by walking out on the discussion. The rabbis consistently provide an apology for Jonah's behavior, explaining it on the basis of his love for Israel. They imagine Jonah as thinking, "Since the heathens are nearer to repentance, I might be causing Israel to be condemned. Rather I would die."[167] The question will be put to Jonah again (4:9), but first there are three further "appointing" acts of the Lord.

What had the prophet been doing since delivering his message to Nineveh? Where had he been? The text does not say; it is not necessary in a story that everything be spelled out.

The word "city" occurs three times in this verse. The theme of the previous scene remains an urgent concern for Jonah and for those who hear or read the story.

The word "booth" (Heb., *sukkāh*) may refer to a temporary shelter for

---

165 See Magonet, *Form,* 56.

166 Often translated as a pluperfect, "and Jonah had gone out," to indicate the setting for the whole scene (Wolff, Rudolph, and others). But an ordinary past tense makes sense, indicating that Jonah reacted to the Lord's question with an act, not with words (cf. Sasson, 287ff.).

167 Cited in LaCocque (p. 138), from *Mekilta,* tractate *Pisha* I, 80–92 (ed. Lauterbach).

cattle (Gen. 33:17) or for soldiers while out in the field (1 Kings 20:12, 16) or for a guard stationed in a vineyard (Isa. 1:8). It also refers to the temporary shelters made of the branches of "olive, wild olive, myrtle, palm, and other leafy trees" (Neh. 8:15) and stationed at various places during the Feast of Booths (*sukkôt*). The purpose was—and remains for Jews today—to provide a dramatic illustration of the way the people of Israel had lived during the time of the wilderness wandering (Lev. 23:42–43; Neh. 8:14–18; cf. also Deut. 16:13, 16; Zech. 14:16, 18, 19).

Jonah still seems to think that some sort of catastrophe might come upon Nineveh, as he sits, waiting "until he should see what happened to the city."

> **6 The LORD God appointed a plant which grew up over Jonah to be shade over his head, to save him from his discomfort. Jonah was very happy because of the plant. 7 Then God appointed a worm at the break of dawn the next day and it attacked the plant and it dried up. 8 When the sun rose God appointed a hot east wind and it attacked Jonah's head and he became faint. He asked that he might die, saying, "It is better for me to die than to live."**

[6] Just as the Lord had appointed a big fish (1:17), so now the story reports three further acts of appointing, each involving a miraculous intervention in nature. The Lord is, after all, "the God of heavens, who made the sea and the dry land" (1:9). First, the Lord appoints a plant to provide better shade for Jonah. If Jonah's hut was indeed like a *sukkāh* built at the time of the feast of *sukkôt,* it would have had walls but a leafy roof which afforded only partial protection from the sun and which would soon dry up. When the plant grew, it provided a more substantial roof.[168] The plant is called a *qiyqayon;* the exact species remains uncertain.[169] The narrator continues to play upon the various senses of *rā'āh,* here translated "discomfort."[170] The prophet is here described as subject to extreme mood swings. Chapter 4:1 said literally that Jonah was "displeased with great displeasure." Now, in a balancing cognate accusative construction for emphasis,[171] he literally "rejoiced with great joy," or "was very happy."

[7] In a second act of appointing, at dawn the next day God commissions "a worm" to attack the plant, which then dries up. Here the name

---

[168] See Gese, 265–266, and the passage in Tractate *Sukkah* 1:1–11 to which he refers.

[169] For a recent discussion, see Robinson, 390–403; Robinson tends toward understanding the plant as a member of the gourd family but concludes that certainty is impossible. Halpern and Friedman (pp. 85–86) suggest that the word sounds like "vomiting of Jonah"; cf. Robinson, 402.

[170] See also 3:8, 10; 4:2.

[171] See note 54 on 1:10.

"God" (*Elohim*) appears; the emphasis is not on God's love and mercy but on God's disciplining activity.[172]

[8]   The third act of appointing involves the sending of "a hot east wind." The meaning of the Hebrew *ḥerîšît* is unknown, but the context requires something like "hot" or "sultry."[173] Jonah is sitting to the east of the city and thus does not benefit from any protection from the wind that the city might afford. Again the storyteller likes to repeat words for effect: just as the worm had "attacked" the plant, so now the sun "attacked" Jonah's head. In Jonah's environment, the hot sun could be a serious threat to well-being (2 Kings 4:18-20 and Judith 8:2-3 report deaths by sunstroke) and one of the Lord's benefits is the providing of shade (Isa. 49:2; Ps. 121:5-6).

The word "faint" also occurs with this sense in Amos 8:13. The words "he asked that he might die" are identical to Elijah's request in 1 Kings 19:4.[174]

"It is better for me to die than to live" repeats Jonah's words in 4:3. The encounters with the plant, the worm, and the wind have not proved to be educational experiences for the prophet. He has not moved beyond his wish to die.

9   Then God said to Jonah, "Is it right for you to be angry because of the plant?" And he said, "It is right for me to be angry enough to die."

[9]   Again, the issue is Jonah's anger. The chapter began by declaring that Jonah was burning with anger. After his initial prayer to the Lord, a prayer consisting of thirty-nine words, the Lord asked him, "Is it right for you to be angry?" (4:4). The question was left hanging, as Jonah went out to the east of the city and as God carried out the three acts of appointing. The death of the plant, which had provided shade for Jonah, evokes another death wish from the prophet. Then, in the same words as 4:4, God asks Jonah whether his anger, set off by the dying of a plant, is justifiable. This time Jonah asserts that he has a right to be angry enough to want to die.

10   Then the Lord said, "You cared about the plant, which you did not work for nor grow; it appeared overnight and died overnight. 11   And I, should I not care about Nineveh, that great city, in which there are more than a hundred and twenty thousand persons who do not know their right hand from their left, and also many animals?"

---

[172] See "The Names for God in Jonah," pp. 45-46 above.

[173] Sasson makes the interesting suggestion that this unusual word was chosen because its consonants echo *haššaḥar* ("dawn") in the previous verse; see his discussion on pp. 302-304.

[174] For further contacts with 1 Kings 19, see the comments on 4:3 and p. 30 above.

[10] The story ends as it began, with a word from the Lord. After this last scene has spoken of the acts and words of "the LORD God" and of "God," this concluding question comes from "the LORD," the name used when the accent is on the Lord's love and concern.[175] The Lord's statement is thirty-nine words in Hebrew, balancing Jonah's speech of thirty-nine words in 4:2.[176]

The Lord points out that Jonah cared deeply about a plant, over which he had not labored and which he had not nurtured. After all, it had appeared overnight and died overnight. The verb "died" recalls the desperate hope of the captain (1:6) and of the king (3:9) that their people not die. Jonah cares deeply about the death of one plant — because its death reduced his own comfort level.

[11] The argument here is of the "how much more" type, familiar in the Bible and in Judaism (Gen. 44:8; Deut. 31:27; 2 Kings 5:13; Matt. 6:30; 10:31; 12:12; Luke 12:24).[177] The Hebrew word order indicates emphasis to stress the change of subject:[178] "And I, should I not . . . ?" The verb translated "care" means literally having tears in one's eyes; "the eye flows on account of."[179] The Lord sees the city of Nineveh and is moved to tears of compassion. The picture of Jesus weeping over the city of Jerusalem comes to mind (Luke 19:41–44; cf. Matt. 23:37; 9:36; Mark 6:34; 8:2).

The city is described quantitatively, in terms of its population size, and then qualitatively, in terms of its needs: "a hundred and twenty thousand who do not know." The people of Nineveh are portrayed as helpless (cf. Amos 7:2, 5), hardly able to distinguish right from left.

The final words in the book are, "and also many animals." The story of Jonah acknowledges a solidarity between humans and the animals. The animals of Nineveh joined in the act of repentance (3:7–8). The word translated "animals" (*behēmāh*) may denote all creatures on earth in contrast to human beings or, in a more restricted sense, domesticated animals or cattle (Gen. 47:18; Ex. 20:10).[180] The narrative ends with this comment about the Lord's care for the cattle grazing on an Assyrian hillside. The reader of the New Testament is reminded of what Jesus said about God's care for the sparrows of Jerusalem: "And not one of them

---

[175] See "The Names for God in Jonah," pp. 45–46 above.

[176] See Magonet, *Form,* 56–57.

[177] This method of argument is called *qal wahomer,* "from minor to major"; see *Encyclopaedia Judaica* (New York: Macmillan, 1971), 8:1421. See also Sasson, 307–308.

[178] See note 30 on 1:4.

[179] KB, 282.

[180] See the comments on 3:7–8.

will fall to the ground without your Father's will. . . . Fear not, therefore; you are of more value than many sparrows" (Matt. 10:29–31, RSV).

If Jonah is a didactic story,[181] a fundamental interpretive question is: What is this biblical book aiming to teach? If it is a didactic story in scripture, the fundamental interpretive question may be focused more sharply: What is this biblical book aiming to teach about God?

Teachers have always relied on questions as a means toward instruction. In this final scene, the Lord puts three questions to Jonah. The first two have to do with Jonah's attitude toward Nineveh, the last with Jonah's attitude toward the Lord's actions with Nineveh. In its present form the book is designed to be read to a gathered community. Just as the words of testimony in scene III (1:17–2:10) are addressed to that community, so this final question is put to each person hearing or reading this book. The question calls forth two pictures: a teeming metropolis, far from Jerusalem and filled with helpless people, and a herd of cattle grazing on a hillside. The Lord asks Jonah, and through Jonah, each person who hears the story: Shouldn't I be concerned about all these people? And about all these cattle as well?

The answer, of course, is "Yes." And that "yes" expresses a unique emphasis in the book of Jonah. The entire Bible tells the story of God's love for the insiders, the people of Israel and the people of the New Testament church. The book of Jonah, however, has a special concern to show God's love for the outsiders, the people of the world — and even for their cattle!

A most memorable exposition of this final statement in the book of Jonah may be seen in the Jonah window in Christ Church Cathedral, in Oxford, England.[182] Jonah is sitting under the plant. His focus — and the focus of the viewer — is on the city of Nineveh. We see the houses, the shops, and the streets, and cannot but recall these words: "Should I not care about Nineveh, that great city . . . ?"

---

[181] See pp. 22ff. above.
[182] Crafted by the van Linge brothers of Emden, Ostfriesland, in 1631.

APPENDIX

The book of Jonah has called forth an amazing response, not only from commentators in the Jewish, Christian, and Muslim communities but also from poets, novelists, musicians, and artists. To offer a complete history of the interpretation of this small book would be not only beyond the capabilities of this writer but also beyond the space limitations of this commentary and no doubt beyond the interest of the reader.

Jonah is mentioned in the canonical Old Testament in 2 Kings 14:25 and in the book bearing his name. The New Testament refers to Jonah in Matt. 12:38–42; 16:1–4; and Luke 11:29–32. What is offered here are some highlights from the continuing history of the interpretation of the book. I have included works that seem to me both interesting and of significance for the task of the present-day interpreter. Since Jonah is the property of the Jewish, Christian, and Islamic communities, examples from all three traditions have been included. When the works are quite easily available, such as those from the apocryphal/deuterocanonical writings and the selections from Charlesworth's *Old Testament Pseudepigrapha*, they have been excerpted. In the case of those pieces which are not so immediately accessible, I have cited them either in complete form (Josephus on Jonah, the Jonah sections from *Pirke de Rabbi Eliezer* and from *The Tales of the Prophets of al-Kisa'i*) or in excerpts as judgment suggests and space permits (from the *Zohar,* the *Midrash Jonah,* and the Koran).

The short essays on Jonah in the works of Luther and Calvin have been included because of the obvious significance of these reformers in the history of biblical interpretation.

1. Jonah in the Apocryphal/Deuterocanonical Books

At the end of the book of Tobit (2nd century B.C.) the aged Tobit, who had been deported to Nineveh after the 722 fall of Samaria, advises his son to leave Nineveh because Jonah had announced the destruction of the city.[1]

---

[1] Tobit 14:4, 8, RSV; see pp. 19, 80 above.

The reference to the "twelve prophets" in Sir. 49:10 indicates that Jonah was a part of the canonical Book of the Twelve during the second century B.C. when Sirach was composed.[2]

Third Maccabees (1st century B.C.) reports a bizarre plan of Ptolemy to eliminate the Jewish population of Alexandria by enclosing them in a hippodrome and having them stampeded by five hundred drugged elephants. In this dire situation, the priest Eleazar offers a prayer in which he recalls five instances of the Lord's saving acts: the rescue from Egypt, from the Assyrians, the deliverance of the three men in the furnace, and of Daniel and Jonah:

> And Jonah, wasting away in the belly of a huge, sea-born monster, you, Father, watched over and restored unharmed to all his family.
> (3 Macc. 6:8)

In a segment to be dated around A.D. 150, 2 Esdras reports God addressing Ezra as the father of the Israelite nation:

> And now, father, look with pride and see the people coming from the east; to them I will give as leaders Abraham, Isaac, and Jacob and Hosea and Amos and Micah and Joel and Obadiah and Jonah and Nahum and Habakkuk, Zephaniah, Haggai, Zechariah and Malachi. . . .
> (2 Esd. 1:38–40)

In these apocryphal/deuterocanonical works, Jonah is regarded as canonical scripture (Sirach). Tobit recalled Jonah's words in Nineveh. In 3 Maccabees, Jonah's deliverance from the whale is ranked with the great deliverances of Israel and of individuals in Israel; a detail is added in the mention of Jonah's family. In a vision of the future, 2 Esdras lists Jonah with the rest of the twelve prophets as well as with the great leaders of Israel.

2. Jonah in Literature from the First Centuries A.D.

1. Josephus reports on Jonah in ch. 10 of *Antiquities of the Jews,* published in the late first century A.D.:

> In the fifteenth year of the reign of Amaziah, Jeroboam the son of Joash reigned over Israel in Samaria forty years. This king was guilty of contumely against God, and became very wicked in worshipping of idols, and in many undertakings that were absurd and foreign. He was also the cause of ten thousand misfortunes to the people of Israel. Now one

---

[2] For the quotation, see p. 20 above.

Jonah, a prophet, foretold to him that he should make war with the Syrians, and conquer their army, and enlarge the bounds of his kingdom on the northern parts, to the city Hamath, and on the southern, to the lake Asphaltitis; for the bounds of the Canaanites orginally were these, as Joshua their general had determined them. So Jeroboam made an expedition against the Syrians, and overran all their country, as Jonah had foretold.

Now I cannot but think it necessary for me, who have promised to give an accurate account of our affairs, to describe the actions of this prophet, so far as I have found them written down in the Hebrew books. Jonah had been commanded by God to go to the kingdom of Nineveh; and, when he was there, to publish it in that city, how it should lose the dominion it had over the nations. But he went not, out of fear: nay, he ran away from God to the city of Joppa, and finding a ship there, he went into it, and sailed to Tarsus, to Cilicia; and upon the rise of a most terrible storm, which was so great that the ship was in danger of sinking, the mariners, the master, and the pilot himself, made prayers and vows, in case they escaped the sea. But Jonah lay still and covered [in the ship,] without imitating anything that the others did; but as the waves grew greater, and the sea became more violent by the winds, they suspected, as is usual in such cases, that some one of the persons that sailed with them was the occasion of this storm, and agreed to discover by lot which of them it was. When they had cast lots, the lot fell upon the prophet; and when they asked him whence he came, and what he had done? he replied, that he was a Hebrew by nation, and a prophet of Almighty God; and he persuaded them to cast him into the sea, if they would escape the danger they were in, for that he was the occasion of the storm which was upon them. Now at the first they durst not do so, as esteeming it a wicked thing to cast a man, who was a stranger, and who had committed his life to them, into such manifest perdition; but at last, when their misfortunes overbore them, and the ship was just going to be drowned, and when they were animated to do it by the prophet himself, and by the fear concerning their own safety, they cast him into the sea; upon which the sea became calm. It is also related that Jonah was swallowed down by a whale, and that when he had been there three days, and as many nights, he was vomited out upon the Euxine Sea, and this alive, and without any hurt upon his body; and there, on his prayer to God, he obtained pardon for his sins, and went to the city Nineveh, where he stood so as to be heard; and preached, that in a very little time they should lose the dominion of Asia; and when he had published this, he returned. Now, I have given this account about him, as I found it written [in our books.][3]

---

[3] Josephus, *Antiquities of the Jews*, in *Complete Works*, trans. W. Whiston (Grand Rapids: Kregel Publications, 1960), 207–208.

"Tarshish" is understood as a reference to Tarsus in Asia Minor. Josephus assumes that carrying a criminal on board could be the cause of a storm, "as is usual in such cases." He introduces the account about the fish with some reserve: "It is also related . . . ." Nothing is reported of Nineveh's reaction to Jonah's preaching or of the events from Jonah 3:5 to the end of the story.

2. The opening lines of the *Lives of the Prophets* (first century A.D.) indicate that this work will provide "the names of the prophets, and where they are from, and where they died and how, and where they lie." The Jonah section reads:

> Jonah was from the district of Kariathmos near the Greek city of Azotus by the sea. And when he had been cast forth by the sea monster and had gone away to Nineveh and had returned, he did not remain in his district, but taking his mother along he sojourned in Sour, a territory (inhabited by) foreign nations; for he said, "So shall I remove my reproach, for I spoke falsely in prophesying against the great city of Nineveh." At that time Elijah was rebuking the house of Ahab, and when he had invoked famine upon the land he fled. And he went and found the widow with her son, for he could not stay with uncircumcised people; and he blessed her. And when her son died, God raised him again from the dead through Elijah, for he wanted to show him that it is not possible to run away from God. And after the famine he arose and went into the land of Judah. And when his mother died along the way, he buried her near Deborah's Oak. And after sojourning in the land of Saraar he died and was buried in the cave of Kenaz, who became judge of one tribe in the days of the anarchy. And he gave a portent concerning Jerusalem and the whole land, that whenever they should see a stone crying out piteously the end was at hand. And whenever they should see all the gentiles in Jersualem, the entire city would be razed to the ground.[4]

This report picks up the story of Jonah after his return from Nineveh. Jonah and his mother live in Sour, a city whose location is not known (cf. Sur, Judith 2:28). In a surprising interpretive move, they are identified as the widow and son visited by Elijah (1 Kings 17:8–16) who was active during the time of Ahab (869–850 B.C.), thus about a hundred years before the time of Jeroboam II (786–746). According to this account, Jonah's reputation as a prophet has suffered because his prophecy concerning Nineveh did not come true. When the widow's son (Jonah) died, God raised him up "to show that it is not possible to run away from God," a lesson that the prophet had presumably already learned after his experience with the great fish.

---

[4] *OTP*, 2:392–393.

3. In two instances in literature from this period, Jonah is included with a list of other prophets, in reports of visions of the future.[5] A portion of the *Martrydom and Ascension of Isaiah* (from the end of the first century A.D.) speaks of the future coming of the Lord. At the conclusion of the discussion, Isaiah says:

> And all these things, behold they are written in the Psalms, in the parables of David the son of Jesse, and in the Proverbs of Solomon his son, and in the words of Korah and of Ethan the Israelite, and in the words of Asaph, and in the rest of the psalms which the angel of the spirit has inspired, (namely) in those which have no name written, and in the words of Amos my father and of Hosea the prophet, and of Micah, and of Joel, and of Nahum, and of Jonah, and of Obadiah, and of Habakkuk, and of Haggai, and of Zephaniah, and of Zechariah, and of Malachi, and in the words of the righteous Joseph, and in the words of Daniel. (4:21–22)[6]

A section of the *Sibylline Oracles* (before A.D. 150) looks forward to the resurrection of the dead:

> Christ, imperishable himself, will come in glory on a cloud toward the imperishable one with the blameless angels. He will sit on the right of the Great One, judging at the tribunal the life of pious men and the way of impious men. Moses, the great friend of the Most High, also will come, having put on flesh. Great Abraham himself will come, Isaac and Jacob, Joshua, Daniel and Elijah, Habakkuk and Jonah, and those whom the Hebrews killed. (2:241–248)[7]

4. Finally, Jonah appears in the context of a number of the prayers in *Hellenistic Synagogal Prayers* (between A.D. 150 and 350) which appear to have been originally Jewish prayers, adapted for use by the Christian community. Prayer 6 recalls how God had accepted the petitions of people in the past and asks that those of the present be accepted:

> Now also, yourself, O Master God,
> accept the entreaties on the lips of your people,
>   who (have come) out of (the) gentiles,
>   who call upon you in truth,
> even as you received the gifts of the righteous in their generations:
>   [The list goes from Abel through Esdra/Ezra, then continues]
>   Daniel in the hole of the lions;
>   Jonah in the belly of the whale;
>   the three children in a furnace of fire. . . .

---

[5] See also the quotation from 2 Esdras cited above (p. 100).
[6] *OTP*, 2:163.
[7] *OTP*, 1:351.

And now, therefore, receive the prayers of your people,
offered up with full knowledge to you through Christ in the Spirit.[8]

The adaptation of these Jewish prayers by the Christian community indicates that such a transition could be quite naturally made. As in 3 Maccabees, Jonah is closely associated with Daniel and those in the fiery furnace.

To summarize: In these writings from the first centuries A.D., Jonah may appear with other prophets and worthies of the Old Testament in visions of the future (*Martyrdom of Isaiah; Sibylline Oracles;* cf. 2 Esdras). In three of these works, that which is remembered about Jonah is his being rescued from the whale (3 Maccabees; *Lives; Synagogal Prayers*). A tendency to elaborate on the story is evident in the *Lives.*

3. Jonah in Judaism

L. Ginzberg has synthesized comments on Jonah from a variety of sources in his collection *The Legends of the Jews.*[9] M. Zlotowitz has prepared a convenient compendium of commentary from traditional Jewish sources.[10] Here are offered considerations of three longer works that evidence themes recurring in further reinterpretations of the Jonah story.

1. *Pirke de Rabbi Eliezer* (The Chapters of Rabbi Eliezer) is a ninth-century work, attributed to Rabbi Eliezer son of Hyrcanos, a figure from the first century A.D.[11] After two chapters introducing Eliezer and telling of his call to become a rabbi, some fifty-one chapters provide comments on events from the work of creation up through the time of Israel's wandering in the wilderness. Chapter 10 retells the events of the biblical Jonah 1–2, and ch. 43 deals with the repentance of Nineveh as described in Jonah 3 and 4:

> On the fifth day Jonah fled before his God. Why did he flee? Because on the first occasion when (God) sent him to restore the border of Israel, his words were fulfilled, as it is said, "And he restored the border of Israel from the entering in of Hamath" (2 Kings xiv.25). On the second occasion (God) sent him to Jerusalem to (prophesy that He would) destroy it. But the Holy One, blessed be He, did according to the abundance of His tender mercy and repented of the evil (decree), and He did not destroy it; thereupon they called him a lying prophet. On

---

[8] *OTP,* 2:684–685.

[9] Philadelphia: Jewish Publication Society, 1946 (vol. 6) and 1947 (vol. 4).

[10] M. Zlotowitz, *Yonah/Jonah: A New Translation with a Commentary Anthologized from Midrashic and Rabbinic Sources* (Brooklyn, N.Y.: Mesorah Publications, 1978).

[11] *Pirkê de Rabbi Eliezer,* trans. and ed. G. Friedlander (New York: Benjamin Blom, 1971).

the third occasion (God) sent him against Nineveh to destroy it. Jonah argued with himself, saying, I know that the nations are nigh to repentance, now they will repent and the Holy One, blessed be He, will direct His anger against Israel. And is it not enough for me that Israel should call me a lying prophet; but shall also the nations of the world (do likewise)? Therefore, behold, I will escape from His presence to a place where His glory is not declared. (If) I ascend above the heavens, it is said, "Above the heavens is his glory" (Ps. cxiii.4). (If) above the earth, (it is said), "The whole earth is full of his glory" (Isa. vi.3); behold, I will escape to the sea, to a place where His glory is not proclaimed. Jonah went down to Joppa, but he did not find there a ship in which he could embark, for the ship in which Jonah might have embarked was two days' journey away from Joppa, in order to test Jonah. What did the Holy One, blessed be He, do? He sent against it a mighty tempest on the sea and brought it back to Joppa. Then Jonah saw and rejoiced in his heart, saying, Now I know that my ways will prosper before me.

He said to the (sailors), We will embark with you. They replied to him, Behold, we are going to the islands of the sea, to Tarshish. He said to them, We will go with you. Now (this) is the custom on all ships that when a man disembarks therefrom he pays his fare; but Jonah, in the joy of his heart, paid his fare in advance, as it is said, "But Jonah rose up to flee unto Tarshish from the presence of the Lord; and he went down to Joppa and found a ship going to Tarshish; so he paid the fare thereof, and went down into it, to go with them" (Jonah i.3).

They had travelled one day's journey, and a mighty tempest on the sea arose against them on their right hand and on their left hand; but the movement of all the ships passing to and fro was peaceful in a quiet sea, but the ship into which Jonah had embarked was in great peril of shipwreck, as it is said, "But the Lord sent out a great wind into the sea, and there was a mighty tempest in the sea, so that the ship was like to be broken" (*ibid.* 4).

Rabbi Chanina said: (Men) of the seventy languages were there on the ship, and each one had his god in his hand, (each one) saying: And the God who shall reply and deliver us from this trouble, He shall be God. They arose and every one called upon the name of his god, but it availed nought. Now Jonah, because of the anguish of his soul, was slumbering and asleep. The captain of the ship came to him, saying, Behold, we are standing betwixt death and life, and thou art slumbering and sleeping; of what people art thou? He answered them, "I am an Hebrew" (*ibid.* 9). (The captain) said to him, Have we not heard that the God of the Hebrews is great? Arise, call upon thy God, perhaps He will work (salvation) for us according to all His miracles which He did for you at the Reed Sea. He answered them, It is on my account that this misfortune has befallen you; take me up and cast me into the sea and the sea will become calm unto you, as it is said, "And he said unto them, Take me up, and cast me forth into the sea; so shall the sea be calm unto you" (*ibid.* 12).

Rabbi Simeon said: The men would not consent to throw Jonah into the sea; but they cast lots among themselves and the lot fell upon Jonah. What did they do? They took all their utensils which were in the ship, and cast them into the sea in order to lighten it for their (safety), but it availed nought. They wanted to return to the dry land, but they were unable, as it is said, "Nevertheless the men rowed hard to get them back to the land; but they could not" (*ibid.* 13). What did they do? They took Jonah and they stood on the side of the ship, saying, God of the world! O Lord! Do not lay upon us innocent blood, for we do not know what sort of person is this man; and he says deliberately, On my account has this misfortune befallen you.

They took him (and cast him into the sea) up to his knee-joints, and the sea-storm abated. They took him up again to themselves and the sea became agitated again against them. They cast him in (again) up to his neck, and the sea-storm abated. Once more they lifted him up in their midst and the sea was again agitated against them, until they cast him in entirely and forthwith the sea-storm abated, as it is said, "So they took up Jonah, and cast him forth into the sea: and the sea ceased from her raging" (*ibid.* 15).

"And the Lord had prepared a great fish to swallow up Jonah" (*ibid.* 17). Rabbi Ṭarphon said: That fish was specially appointed from the six days of Creation to swallow up Jonah, as it is said, "And the Lord *had* prepared a great fish to swallow up Jonah" (*ibid.*). He entered its mouth just as a man enters the great synagogue, and he stood (therein). The two eyes of the fish were like windows of glass giving light to Jonah.

Rabbi Meir said: One pearl was suspended inside the belly of the fish and it gave illumination to Jonah, like this sun which shines with its might at noon; and it showed to Jonah all that was in the sea and in the depths, as it is said, "Light is sown for the righteous" (Ps. xcvii.11).

The fish said to Jonah, Dost thou not know that my day had arrived to be devoured in the midst of Leviathan's mouth? Jonah replied, Take me beside it, and I will deliver thee and myself from its mouth. It brought him next to the Leviathan. (Jonah) said to the Leviathan, On thy account have I descended to see thy abode in the sea, for, moreover, in the future will I descend and put a rope in thy tongue, and I will bring thee up and prepare thee for the great feast of the righteous. (Jonah) showed it the seal of our father Abraham (saying), Look at the Covenant (seal), and Leviathan saw it and fled before Jonah a distance of two days' journey. (Jonah) said to it (*i.e.* the fish), Behold, I have saved thee from the mouth of Leviathan, show me what is in the sea and in the depths. It showed him the great river of the waters of the Ocean, as it is said, "The deep was round about me" (Jonah ii.5), and it showed him the paths of the Reed Sea through which Israel passed, as it is said, "The reeds were wrapped about my head" (*ibid.*); and it showed him the place whence the waves of the sea and its billows flow, as it is said, "All thy waves and thy billows passed over me" (*ibid.* 3); and it showed him the pillars of the earth in its foundations, as it is said, "The earth with her bars *for the world* were by me" (*ibid.* 6); and it showed him the lowest Sheol, as it is said, "Yet hast thou brought up my life from destruction, O Lord, my God" (*ibid.*); and it showed him Gehinnom, as it is said, "Out of the belly of Sheol I cried, and thou didst hear my voice" (*ibid.* 2); and it showed him (what was) beneath the Temple of God, as it is said, "(I went down) to the bottom of the mountains" (*ibid.* 6). Hence we may learn that Jerusalem stands upon seven (hills), and he saw there the Eben Shethiyah (Foundation Stone) fixed in the depths. He saw there the sons of Korah standing and praying over it. They said to Jonah, Behold thou dost stand beneath the Temple of God, pray and thou wilt be answered. Forthwith Jonah said to the fish, Stand in the place where thou art standing, because I wish to pray. The fish stood (still), and Jonah began to pray before the Holy One, blessed be He, and he said: Sovereign of all the Universe! Thou art called "the One who kills" and "the One who makes alive," behold, my soul has reached unto death, now restore me to life. He was not answered until this word came forth from his mouth, "What I have vowed I will perform" (*ibid.* 9), namely, I vowed to draw up Leviathan and to prepare it before Thee, I will perform (this) on the day of the Salvation of Israel, as it is said, "But I will sacrifice unto thee with the voice of thanksgiving" (*ibid.*). Forthwith the Holy One, blessed be He, hinted (to the fish) and it vomited out Jonah upon the dry land, as it is said, "And the Lord spake unto the fish, and it vomited out Jonah upon the dry land" (*ibid.* 10).

The sailors saw all the signs, the miracles, and the great wonders which the Holy One, blessed be He, did unto Jonah, and they stood and they cast away every one his God, as it is said, "They that regard lying vanities forsake their own shame" (*ibid.* 8). They returned to Joppa and went up to Jerusalem and circumcised the flesh of their foreskins, as it is said, "And the men feared the Lord exceedingly; and they offered a sacrifice unto the Lord" (*ibid.* i.16). Did they offer sacrifice? But this (sacrifice) refers to the blood of the covenant of circumcision, which is like the blood of a sacrifice. And they made vows every one to bring his children and all belonging to him to the God of Jonah; and they made vows and performed them, and concerning them it says, "Upon the proselytes, the proselytes of righteousness."[12]

Chapter 43, "The Power of Repentance," describes the repentance of Nineveh as reported in Jonah 3 with some imaginative embellishment.[13]

In sum, this retelling of the Jonah story provides a creative example of

---

[12] *PRE,* 65–73.
[13] See p. 87 above.

the application of biblical texts to the contemporary situation. The prophet is portrayed in a more positive light: Jonah avoids going to Nineveh because he suspects the Ninevites will repent, which would make Israel look bad. Miraculous elements are heightened: the Lord sends a storm to bring the Joppa ship back to the harbor; the storm affects only Jonah's ship. The biblical story is elaborated upon: the crew is made up of men of the seventy nations of the world; Jonah is gradually dipped into the water; Jonah's stay in the fish is described with great imagination. The problem of offering sacrifices away from the temple is dealt with: the sailors all go to Jerusalem. The story is cut off after the events of Jonah 2, though the theme of the repentance of Nineveh is taken up in *Pirke,* ch. 43.

2. In the *Zohar,*[14] in the course of a commentary on Ex. 35:1–38:20, Rabbi Abba offers a discourse on Jonah 2:10: "And the Lord (had) said unto the fish, and it vomited out Jonah upon the dry land."

"Where and when did God speak to the fish?" he asked. "It was," he replied, "at the time of Creation, when the Holy One, blessed be He, created the world; to wit, on the fifth day, when He created the fishes of the sea. Then He ordained and appointed a certain fish to swallow up Jonah and retain him in its body three days and three nights and then eject him. . . . On the fifth day He created the fishes of the sea and the birds of heaven. With the birds he stipulated that they should feed Elijah when he restrained the heaven from rain, as it is written: "and I have commanded the ravens to feed thee there" (I Kings 17:4); and He stipulated with the fishes of the sea to appoint one fish that should swallow up Jonah and then eject him. On the sixth day He created Adam and stipulated with him that a woman should descend from him who should sustain Elijah, as it is written, "Behold I have commanded a widow there to sustain thee" (*Ibid.* 17:9). Similarly, in regard to every unique phenomenon that has happened in the world, the Holy One, blessed be He, had predestined it from the time when the world was created. And so here the meaning of "And the Lord said to the fish" is that He had commanded it at the creation of the world.

In the story of Jonah we have a representation of the whole of a man's career in this world. Jonah descending into the ship is symbolic of man's soul that descends into this world to enter into his body. Why is she [the soul] called Jonah (lit. aggrieved) [one possible understanding of the Hebrew]? Because as soon as she becomes partner with the body in this world she finds herself full of vexation. Man, then, is in this world as in a ship that is traversing the great ocean and is like to be broken, as it says, "so that the ship was like to be broken" (Jonah 1:4). Furthermore, man in this world commits sins, imagining that he can flee from the presence of his Master, who takes no notice of this world. The

[14] Trans. M. Simon and P. P Levertoff (London: Soncino Press, 1934), 4:172–176.

Almighty then rouses a furious tempest; to wit, man's doom, which constantly stands before the Holy One, blessed be He, and demands his punishment. It is this which assails the ship and calls to mind man's sins that it may seize him; and the man is thus caught by the tempest and struck down by illness, just as Jonah "went down into the innermost part of the ship; and he lay, and was fast asleep." Although the man is thus prostrated, his soul does not exert itself to return to his Master in order to make good his omissions.

The allegory continues:

For the fish that swallowed him is, in fact, the grave; and so "Jonah was in the belly of the fish," which is identified with "the belly of the underworld" (*Sheol*), as is proved by the passage, "Out of the belly of the underworld (*sheol*) cried I."

Then Rabbi Abba moves toward a conclusion by coming back to the text (Jonah 2:10 [11]), understanding Jonah's being spit out as a reference to the resurrection of the dead:

Thus in the narrative of that fish we find words of healing for the whole world. As soon as it swallowed Jonah it died, but after three days was restored to life and vomited him forth. In a similar way the Land of Israel will in the future be stirred to new life, and afterwards "the earth will cast forth the dead."

Here is quite a different interpretation of Jonah. The discourse is based on Jonah 1 and 2. The story of Jonah becomes every person's story, from the time the soul enters the body and makes its way through the storms of life until death and the grave. But just as Jonah was spit out by the fish, humans will be ejected from the grave into a new life.

3. The first part of the *Midrash Jonah* runs parallel to the *Pirke de Rabbi Eliezer* for the first two chapters of Jonah.[15] There are a few interesting additions, not found in *PRE*. Jonah 1:2 reports that the prophet fled to Tarshish. The Midrash asks, "With what can this be compared?" The answer:

To a king of flesh and blood, whose wife died as she was nursing their son. He looked for a wet nurse to nurse his son, so that he would not die. What did the king's wet nurse do? She left the king's son lying in bed and ran away. When the king saw that she had run away and had left his son lying in bed, he wrote a letter, commanding that she be captured and thrown into prison, in a place where there were snakes and scorpions. After a few days the king went to the pit where she was imprisoned, and she wept and called to the king from the pit. Then the

---

[15] August Wünsche, *Aus Israels Lehrhallen,* vol. 2 (Hildesheim: Georg Olms, 1967), 39–56.

king was moved to have mercy, and he ordered his servants to pull her out and bring her before him. So it was also with Jonah. When he fled from the Holy One, blessed be He, He put him in the belly of a fish until he cried to the Holy One, blessed be He, and the fish threw him out.[16]

Another detail that is not found in *PRE:* According to Rabbi Jochanan, Jonah paid the fare for all the passengers on board.[17]

The Midrash includes a lengthy account about Jonah's sojourn in a second fish, one that was pregnant:[18]

Jonah had been three days in the belly of the fish and had not prayed. Then the Holy One, blessed be He, spoke: "I have made a roomy place for him in the belly of the fish, so that he does not become anxious, and he is not praying to me. Now I will appoint a pregnant fish that has 365,000 small fish in it, so that he will become afraid and pray to me, because I desire the prayers of the righteous."

In this hour the Holy One, blessed be He, apppointed a pregnant fish and she went to the fish [carrying Jonah] and said to it: "The Holy One, blessed be He, sent me to swallow the man, the prophet, that is in your body. It would be good if you would spit him out; if not, I will swallow you with him."

The fish [carrying Jonah] spoke to the pregnant fish, "Who knows whether what you say is true."

She answered, "Leviathan knows it." So they both went to Leviathan. The pregnant fish said to Leviathan, "O King of the fish of the waters, do you not know that the Holy One, blessed be He, has sent the prophet that is in his body, to be swallowed?"

"Yes indeed!" answered Leviathan.

"When did you learn this?" asked the pregnant fish.

"In the last three hours. As the Holy One, blessed be He, came to play with me, I heard that He said to the pregnant fish: 'Go and swallow the prophet who is in the body of the fish.'"

Immediately the fish spit Jonah out, and the pregnant fish swallowed him. As he went into her belly, he was very much afraid because of the dirt and refuse from all the fish. He immediately lifted his heart in prayer before the Holy One, blessed be He: "and Jonah prayed to the Eternal One, his God, from the belly of the fish" (Jonah 2:2).[19]

The Midrash concludes with an account of the sailors going to Jerusalem and being circumcised. The story continues with a description of Nineveh:

---

[16] Wünsche, 39 (my translation).

[17] Wünsche, 40.

[18] For the reason for introducing this pregnant fish, see pp. 112–113 below.

[19] Wünsche, 43–44 (my translation).

"But Nineveh was a large city." Nineveh was 40 parasangs square. In it were 12 streets, in every street were 12,000 people, and every street had two marketplaces, and every marketplace had 12 corridors, and every corridor had 12 courts, and every court had 12 houses, and in every house were 12 strong men, and every strong man had 12 sons. And Jonah stood on one of the streets and called out, and his voice carried for 40 parasangs, so that one could hear his voice in every corridor, in every court, in every house, and in every gate of the city of Nineveh.[20]

The repentance of the people is elaborated upon:

They lifted their nursing infants toward heaven and spoke to the Holy One, praised be He, with great weeping: "Do it for the sake of these, who have never sinned." Perhaps the Holy One, praised be He, will have mercy on us and keep us from being destroyed because of His anger. According to Rabbi ben Chalaftha the people of Nineveh carried out a deceptive kind of repentance. What did they do? They placed calves inside their houses and their mothers outside, so that the calves cried and howled inside and the cows outside. The people said to the Holy One, blessed be He! If you do not have mercy on us, we will not have mercy on these.[21]

The Midrash gives a number of concrete examples to show how the people of Nineveh repented. Among these:

If someone [in Nineveh] sold an old house to another person, and the one who bought it went inside and began to restore it, and found a treasure of silver and gold, what did he do? He called the man, who had sold him the old house, and said: "The treasure that I found in the house belongs to you." But the seller answered the buyer, "When I sold you the old house, I sold it to you with everything that was in it; anything hidden belongs to you." Because neither one would keep the treasure, neither the seller nor the buyer, both went to the judge. The buyer said to the judge, "Your honor, when I bought this old house from this man, I bought only the old house. When I looked in it, I found jewels and pearls. Now he should take these from me and not leave them with me, because the Holy One, praised be He! destroys the world because of robbers, as it says: 'The earth is full of violence because of them'" (Gen. 6:3). The seller spoke again to the judge: "When I sold this house to him, I sold it with everything in it; just as you run away from robbery, so also do I run from robbery, because everyone who robs his neighbor, even if it is just so much as one peruta, is as if his soul had been taken away from him, as it says in Proverbs 1:19 'Such is the end of all

---

[20] Wünsche, 45–46 (my translation).
[21] Wünsche, 46–47 (my translation).

who are greedy for gain; it takes away the life of its possessors.'" What did the judge do? He called for the documents for the house, investigated four generations back and then found the heir of that man who had hidden the treasure and gave it to him as the rightful owner, as it says in Psalm 85:11: "Faithfulness will spring up from the ground, and righteousness will look down from the sky." When the Holy One, praised be He! saw the people of Nineveh and their good works, He called off His sentence of judgment.[22]

The Midrash continues with more reflections on fasting:

Our rabbis taught: What is the procedure for fasting? The ark (with the tables of the law) is brought to the center of the marketplace. People put ashes from the furnace on the ark, and on the head of the prince, and on the head of the president of the court, and every individual takes ashes and puts them on his head, and the eldest among them says to them the following humbling words: "Our brothers! (from the people of Nineveh we have learned) that sackcloth and fasting do not bring about (forgiveness), but repentance and good works, as it says: 'When God saw what they did, how they turned from their evil ways . . .'" (Jonah 3:10).[23]

Another example:

Samuel said: "Even when someone had robbed a two-by-four and had used it in a building, he tore the building down and gave it back to its owner."[24]

Why did Jonah get so angry with God, so that he could say, "It is better for me to die than to live"? The Midrash provides an answer:

Because of the great heat in the belly of the pregnant fish, Jonah's clothing, his jacket, and his hair were burned up, and flies, mosquitoes, ants, and flees settled on him and made him so miserable that he wished he were dead.[25]

The second part of the Midrash picks up the allegory of Jonah in the ship as representing the human soul in the world, as found in the *Zohar*.[26]

This retelling of the Jonah story once again illustrates how imagination can elaborate upon the biblical text and apply it to a contemporary situation. This elaboration may grow out of serious attention to the details of the biblical text. For example, the noun "fish" in 1:17 is masculine, in 2:1

---

[22] Wünsche, 47–48 (my translation).

[23] Wünsche, 49 (my translation).

[24] Wünsche, 50 (my translation).

[25] Wünsche, 50 (my translation).

[26] See the previous section.

feminine. In order to explain this detail, the Midrash develops the scene where Jonah finds himself in the womb of a second fish. The great monster Leviathan reports that "the Holy One, blessed be He, came to play with me," recalling Job 41:5. Or the elaboration may be developed freely, without biblical connection, as in the description of Nineveh or the explanation for Jonah's anger.

The didactic aims of the storyteller are apparent: Once one has been saved from danger, it is easy to forget to pray; thus the move from one fish to another. The story about the treasure in the house puts a high value on integrity, here exemplified by foreigners! The description of fasting makes the point that repentance is not just a matter of externals.

The retellings of the Jonah story by Rabbi Eliezer, in the *Zohar,* and in this Midrash, all provide examples of the creative application of biblical texts to contemporary situations. Fantasy is allowed free reign, but it is a fantasy that is rooted in the biblical tradition. The interpreter may spin out somewhat exotic variations, but these variations always eventually return to the text (*Zohar*). The elaborations on the biblical story are like counterpoint that is freely developed but that always remains related to the cantus firmus, or like a flag waving to and fro but that remains anchored to the flagpole. If this is the sort of teaching that took place "in Israel's classrooms," to pick up the title from Wünsche's collection, those classrooms must have been filled with wonder and laughter as well as with learning.

4. Jonah in Islam

1. Jonah, according to the *First Encyclopaedia of Islam,* is the only one of the major and minor prophets to be mentioned in the Koran.[27] He may be listed with those who have been inspired by God:

Behold, We[28] have inspired thee [O Prophet] just as We inspired Noah and all the prophets after him — as We inspired Abraham, and Ishmael, and Isaac, and Jacob, and their descendants, including Jesus and Job, and Jonah, and Aaron, and Solomon; and as We vouchsafed unto David a book of divine wisdom. (4:163)[29]

Jonah is among those who have received divine guidance:

---

[27] *First Encyclopaedia of Islam,* ed. M. Th. Houtsma et al. (Leiden: E. J. Brill, 1987), 8:1175–1176.

[28] "We" refers to God in these passages.

[29] Citations of the Koran are from *The Message of the Qur'ān,* translated and explained by Muhammad Asad (Gibraltar: Dar al-Andalus, 1980).

And We bestowed upon him Isaac and Jacob; and We guided each of them as We had guided Noah aforetime. And out of his offspring, [We bestowed prophethood upon] David, and Solomon, and Job, and Joseph, and Moses, and Aaron: for thus do We reward the doers of good; and [upon] Zachariah, and John, and Jesus, and Elijah: every one of them was of the righteous; and [upon] Ishmael, and Elisha, and Jonah, and Lot. And every one of them did We favour above other people. (6:84–86)

Sura 10 is called Yunus, or Jonah. The people of Nineveh are held up as exemplary for their faith:

For, alas, there has never yet been any community that attained to faith [in its entirety,] and thereupon benefited by its faith, except the people of Jonah. When they came to believe, We removed from them the suffering of disgrace [which otherwise would have befallen them even] in the life of this world, and allowed them to enjoy their life during the time allotted to them. (10:98)

Jonah may be called "him of the great fish":

And [remember] him of the great fish — when he went off in wrath, thinking that We had no power over him! But then he cried out in the deep darkness [of his distress]: "There is no deity save Thee! Limitless art Thou in Thy glory! Verily, I have done wrong!"
And so We responded unto him and delivered him from [his] distress: for thus do We deliver all who have faith. (21:87–88)
Bear, then, with patience thy Sustainer's will, and be not like him of the great fish, who cried out [in distress] after having given in to anger. [And remember:] had not grace from his Sustainer reached him, he would indeed have been cast forth upon that barren shore in a state of disgrace: but [as it was,] his Sustainer had elected him and placed him among the righteous. (68:48–50)

The Koran also presents an abbreviated version of the entire Jonah story:

And, behold, Jonah was indeed one of Our message-bearers when he fled like a runaway slave onto a laden ship.
And then they cast lots, and he was the one who lost; [and they cast him into the sea,] whereupon the great fish swallowed him, for he had been blameworthy. And had he not been of those who [even in the deep darkness of their distress are able to] extol God's limitless glory, he would indeed have remained in its belly till the Day when all shall be raised from the dead: but We caused him to be cast forth on a desert shore, sick [at heart] as he was, and caused a creeping plant to grow over him [out of the barren soil].
And [then] We sent him [once again] to [his people,] a hundred

thousand [souls] or more: and [this time] they believed [in him] — and so We allowed them to enjoy their life during the time allotted to them. (37:139–148)

This version focuses on two aspects of the Jonah story: the deliverance from the fish and the importance of Jonah's missionary work. Once again, the people of Nineveh are held up as exemplary because of their faith (10:98).[30]

2. *The Tales of the Prophets of al-Kisa'i* is a collection of oral interpretations of stories from the Old and New Testaments, written in Arabic around A.D. 1200.[31]

The story begins by telling of the birth, early childhood, and marriage of Jonah. The second part tells of Jonah's journey to Nineveh:

There was in the city of Nineveh a king called Thaalab ibn Sharid, a haughty tyrant who had raided the Israelites, killing many of them and taking captive a group of them.

God spoke to Jonah, saying, "I have chosen thee as a prophet to the city of Nineveh."

"Send someone else," said Jonah.

"Jonah!" cried God, "Go and do what thou hast been commanded to do and disobey not my command!"

Jonah took his household and children, and having reached the bank of the Tigris, took his elder son across the river and placed him on the bank. Then, while returning to take his younger son, all the possessions that he had with him sank. A wolf came to his elder son and carried him off. Jonah began to run after the wolf, but it turned to him and said intelligibly, "Jonah, turn back from me, for I am commanded so to do." Jonah returned sorrowfully to the bank of the Tigris, but could not find his wife.

God spoke to him, saying, "Thou didst complain of the burden of family, so I have relieved thee of that. Now go and do what thou hast been commanded to do, and then I shall restore thy family and belongings to thee."

Jonah walked to Nineveh, where, in the midst of the city, he cried out in a loud voice, "Confess that there is no god but God and that I, Jonah, am His servant and messenger!" But the people beat him and cursed him, and they only increased in their disbelief and pride. Jonah preached to them for forty days, and they declared him mad.

Then God spoke to him, saying, "Go out from among them, for they will not believe until they experience torment." So he went away from them and sat on a high hill to watch the descent of the punishment upon

---

[30] For a sympathetic analysis of the Jonah material in the Koran, see S. Schreiner, "Muhammads Rezeption der biblischen Jona-Erzählung," *Judaica* 34 (1978): 149–172.

[31] Trans. W. M. Thackston, Jr. (Boston: Twayne Publishers, 1978).

them. And God spoke to Gabriel, saying, "Descend to Malik, the Warden of Hell, and command him to cause sparks to issue forth from Hutama to Jonah's people." Gabriel did as God had commanded, and Malik sent forth sparks the size of thunderclouds.

With that, the king arose and rent his fine robes, ordering his people to do likewise. This they did, weeping and crying out in loud voices, "O God of Jonah, forgive us! We repent to thee, O Most Merciful!"

God accepted their repentance and lifted the punishment from them, but Jonah grew angry and said, "O God, they have denied me, and thou hast pardoned them. Why should I return to them?"

He saw a ship about to set sail and said, "Take me with you." When they took him on board with them, the winds churned up the sea about them and they almost sank. They began to pray, but Jonah kept silent. The people on the ship asked him, "Why do you not pray with us?"

"Because I have lost my wife and children," he answered.

"Then," they said, "there is no doubt that this is because of you, Jonah." They cast lots, and they fell against him; but they said, "The lots fall and may be mistaken. Let us cast names upon the sea." So each one wrote his name on a lead ball and threw it into the sea. The ball of each except Jonah sank, but his name appeared on the surface of the water.

Then a great fish appeared with its mouth open and cried out, "Jonah, I have come from India in search of you." Jonah threw himself into the sea, and the fish swallowed him up and took him first to the Mediterranean and then to the Coral Castle.

The length of time he was in the fish's belly has been disputed: some have said forty days, but Muhammad ibn Jaafar al-Sadiq said only three days.

Then God commanded the fish to cast him out onto the bank of the Tigris, where it cast him out; and he emerged from the fish's belly like a featherless chick, for he was no more than skin and bones and had no strength to stand or to sit, and his vision had gone.

God caused a gourd plant with four branches to grow over him; and Gabriel came to him and rubbed his hand over Jonah's body, causing his skin and flesh to grow again. His sight too was restored. Then God sent a gazelle to give him milk as a mother does to her child. Under the plant was also a spring in which he made his ablutions and the water of which he drank. He remained thus for forty days.

When he awoke from his sleep and saw that the tree had dried up and the gazelle had departed, he wept.

God spoke to him, saying, "Jonah, thou weepest over a gourd and a gazelle, but thou dost not weep over a hundred thousand of my servants!"

Then Jonah traveled back among his people and entered a village with many trees and fruits, which the people were uprooting and casting onto the ground.

"Good people," said Jonah, "why are you destroying these fruits?"

God spoke to him, saying, "Jonah, thou feelest sorry for the fruit tree, but thou dost not feel sorry for my people!"

Then he went to another village, where a potter took him into his house. God spoke to him saying, "Jonah, order him to break his pottery!"

When Jonah told the man to do this, he said, "I received you as a guest tonight because I thought you were a pious man, but you are a fool with no intelligence to order me to break the pottery that I have made. Go away from me!" And the man turned him out of his house in the middle of the night.

God then spoke to him, saying, "Thou didst tell the potter what thou didst tell him, and he put thee out of his house, yet thou wishest the destruction of a hundred thousand and more!"

Rising the next morning and setting out on his way, he found a man sowing, who said to Jonah, "Pray to God that my crop be blessed." He prayed and the crop at once grew up waist high. The man took Jonah to his house and honored him as a guest. And God spoke to him, saying, "I shall send locusts upon this man's crops to eat them up."

"My God," said Jonah, "thou didst answer my prayer for the crops and now thou wishest to destroy them?"

And God spoke to him saying, "O Jonah, thou feelest sorry for crops thou hast not sown, but thou dost not feel sorry for my faithful people!"

"My Lord and Master," he said, "I shall not do it again!"

He came to another village, where he found a man crying out, "Whoever will take this woman to the city of Nineveh to her husband, Jonah son of Matthew, will have a hundred dinars." Jonah at once recognized his wife and said, "Tell me about this woman."

"She was seated on the bank of the Tigris. The lord of this village noticed her and took her off to his castle, where he attempted to entice her to sin, but his hands withered. He asked her to pray God that he be comforted and he would never again approach her; so she prayed and God pardoned him. Then he asked her about her husband, and she said that she was the wife of Jonah son of Matthew. He sent her to me and gave me this gold for her and for the expense of transporting her to her husband."

"I will take her," said Jonah; and the man gave him the woman and the gold.

They walked on together and entered another village, where there was a man selling fish. Jonah bought one and, when he cut open its belly, found all his wealth inside.

Then he saw a man riding an ox, and behind him was a young boy, whom Jonah recognized as his younger son.

"I am Jonah son of Matthew," he said to the man. As the boy greeted his father, Jonah asked what had happened to him.

"I am a fisherman," said the man. "I cast my net into the sea, and this boy fell into it. I found him still alive, and he told me he was the son of Jonah son of Matthew."

Then they went along until they came upon a shepherd watching his flocks. Jonah recognized him as his elder son, and the boy recognized him.

"Father," said the boy, "these sheep belong to a man from this village; come with me so that I can take them back to him." They all went to the owner of the sheep, who, when he heard that the shepherd-boy had found his father Jonah, rejoiced for him and said, "One day I was grazing my sheep when suddenly a wolf approached with this boy and spoke to me in an eloquent tongue, saying, 'This boy is given in trust to you by God.' I took him with devotion; now receive your son safe and sound."

They all went to Jonah's own city, and when the people there saw him they rejoiced. He remained among them, exhorting them to do justice and chastising them for evil, until he died.

Here again is an example of how the Jonah story could be elaborated upon and retold, in this instance in Arabic and in the Muslim world. The biblical story is obviously in the background but the miraculous is heightened: one hears of lead balls that float, of a talking wolf and fish, of nature miracles, the loss and miraculous return of Jonah's family and wealth. The point of the story is clear. Once Jonah repents of his attitude of hatred for the people of Nineveh, all goes well for him. It is also clear that the aim of this retelling of the Jonah story is not only to instruct but also to entertain.

5. Jonah and the Reformers

1. Luther's comments on Jonah are available in English in two versions, one based on Latin lectures given in 1525 and the other on a longer and very popular (going through some fourteen editions) German version first published in 1526.[32] At that time, Luther was involved in controversies with the Enthusiasts. In the midst of these struggles, he thought it important to return to study of the scripture:

For some time I have entered the lists and fought against these spirits and factions. Now that others have joined the fray, I have decided to take Scripture in hand again to feast our hearts, to strengthen, to comfort, and to arm them, lest fatigue and lassitude subdue us in our daily struggle. . . . I have therefore chosen to expound the holy prophet

---

[32] Luther, *Jonah, Habakkuk,* ed. H. C. Oswald, Luther's Works 19 (St. Louis: Concordia Publishing House, 1974).

Jonah, for he is indeed well suited for this situation and represents an
excellent, outstanding, and comforting example of faith and a mighty
and wonderful sign of God's goodness to all the world.[33]

Luther has a keen sense for the story itself and retells it with dramatic
imagination. Discussing Jonah's stay in the fish, Luther says:

> Jonah must have thought these the longest days and nights ever lived
> under the sun. It must have seemed an interminably long time that he
> sat there in the dark. Yes, I suppose that he occasionally lay down and
> stood up. He saw neither sun nor moon and was unable to compute
> the passage of time. Nor did he know where in the sea he was traveling
> about with the fish. How often lung and liver must have pained him!
> How strange his abode must have been among the intestines and the
> huge ribs![34]

We may note the following features of Luther's exposition.

First, Luther understands the Jonah book as a story of God's love for
all people, including for Jonah! He names the story "a mighty and wonderful sign of God's goodness to all the world" and "a comforting illustration
of God's mercy."[35] Luther refers to Jonah as

> a queer and odd saint who is angry because of God's mercy for sinners,
> begrudging them all benefits and wishing them all evil. . . . And yet he
> is God's dear child. He chats so uninhibitedly with God as though he
> were not in the least afraid of Him — as indeed he is not; he confides
> in Him as in a father.[36]

Commenting on God's decision not to destroy Nineveh, Luther says:

> This is a wonderfully sweet expression of the Divine Majesty; this is
> a very complete promise of the incomprehensible goodness and mercy
> of God. This shows how much God does not desire the death of a
> sinner; He desires rather that the sinner be converted and live (cf.
> Ezek. 33:11).[37]

This mercy is for all, Gentiles as well as Jews:

> We have here again an outstanding example of the thing St. Paul is talk-
> ing about in Rom. 3:29: "Is God the God of the Jews only? Is He not
> the God of the Gentiles also? Yes, of the Gentiles also."[38]

---

[33] Luther, *Jonah,* 35–36.
[34] Luther, *Jonah,* 68.
[35] Luther, *Jonah,* 36, 51.
[36] Luther, *Jonah,* 92.
[37] Luther, *Jonah,* 30.
[38] Luther, *Jonah,* 4.

Second, Luther sees the story of Jonah as a testimony to the power of the preached word. He writes:

> If we will think about this account in terms of the power and effect of the Word, the story becomes wonderful and full of comfort. . . . Is not the power of this preaching truly great which within three or four days has converted that very powerful nation with the result that it drives the king and all the inhabitants into ashes, repentant for the sin that was revealed by the Word?[39]

Luther observes that the king of Nineveh did not actually hear Jonah's preaching but only a report about it:

> In view of this, I am tempted to say that no apostle or prophet, not even Christ Himself, performed and accomplished with a single sermon the great things Jonah did. His conversion of the city of Nineveh with one sermon is surely as great a miracle as his rescue from the belly of the whale, if not an even greater one.[40]

Third, Luther understands Jonah as a story that is rich in contemporary relevance. In expositing Jonah 1, for example, he writes:

> All of this is recorded as a warning for us. From it we glean the lesson first of all that he who will not obey God's will willingly must, in the end, bow to His will unwillingly. . . . In the second place, we must learn to know God's mercy well and not depend on our works, whether good or bad, but know that sin does not condemn us nor good works save us, but that only God's grace preserves us.[41]

The application can be very personal, as with 1:9:

> From this let us learn the real art and skill of extricating ourselves from all distress and fear. To do this, we must first of all take note of our sin, forthwith make a clean breast of it, and confess it.[42]

We conclude with a remark Luther made at his table in January of 1538:

> But this story of the prophet Jonah is so great that it is almost unbelievable, yes it even sounds like a lie, and more full of nonsense than any poet's fable. If it were not in the Bible, I'd consider it a silly lie. Because if one thinks about it, Jonah was three days in the huge belly of the whale, where he could have been digested in three hours and changed into the flesh and blood of the whale. He could have died

---

[39] Luther, *Jonah,* 4.
[40] Luther, *Jonah,* 37.
[41] Luther, *Jonah,* 46.
[42] Luther, *Jonah,* 63.

there a hundred times, under the earth, in the sea, inside the whale. Isn't that living in the midst of death? In comparison with this miracle, the wonder at the Red Sea was nothing.[43]

2. Calvin's exposition of Jonah is in the form of a series of nine lectures that were in turn a part of a larger lecture series dealing with the minor prophets.[44] It is clear that Calvin is addressing a real audience. He might comment, "But I cannot now pursue the subject, I must therefore defer it until tomorrow."[45] Each lecture is concluded with a prayer that gathers up the main point of the day's section, summarizes it, and applies it to the audience. For example, after the exposition of 1:7–12:

> Grant, Almighty God, that as thou urgest us daily to repentance . . . , O grant, that we may not grow stupid in our vices, nor deceive ourselves with empty flatteries, but that each of us may, on the contrary, carefully examine his own life, and then with one mouth and heart confess that we are all guilty, not only of light offences, but of such as deserve eternal death, and that no other relief remains for us but thine infinite mercy, and that we may so seek to become partakers of that grace which has been once offered to us by thy Son, and is daily offered to us by his Gospel.[46]

Calvin begins his exposition with a reference to the mention of Jonah in 2 Kings 14. He concludes that Jonah was already active teaching among the people of Israel when he received a command to go to Nineveh:

> The word of God then was not for the first time communicated to Jonah, when he was sent to Nineveh; but it pleased God, when he was already a Prophet, to employ him among other nations.[47]

The nine lectures break the material as follows: 1:1–3, 4–7, 8–12, 13–17; 2:1–7; 2:8–3:5; 3:6–9; 4:1–4; 4:5–11. Calvin thus spent four days on the first chapter, one and one half each on chs. 2 and 3, and two days on ch. 4.

The following themes emerge from Calvin's exposition:

Calvin emphasizes that God is in control of the events of history and nature. Thus when the sailors try to save Jonah (1:13), Calvin says "the Lord so turned their hearts, that they now saw more clearly how grievous

---

[43] *D. Martin Luthers Werke. Tischreden,* vol. 3 (Weimar: Hermann Böhlhaus Nachfolger, 1914), 551 (my translation).

[44] John Calvin, *Commentaries on the Twelve Minor Prophets,* trans. John Owen, vol. 3 (Grand Rapids: Baker Book House, 1979).

[45] Calvin, *Minor Prophets,* 44.

[46] Calvin, *Minor Prophets,* 57–58.

[47] Calvin, *Minor Prophets,* 20.

a sin it was to flee away from the call of God."[48] In regard to the worm
in ch. 4:

> We see here also, that what seemed to happen by chance was yet directed
> by the hidden providence of God. . . . It is yet ever true that the gnaw-
> ings even of worms are directed by the counsel of God, so that neither
> a herb nor a tree withers independently of his purpose. The same truth
> is declared by Christ when he says, that without the Father's appoint-
> ment the sparrows fall not on the ground. . . . Thus much as to the
> worm.[49]

Though God is active in both history and nature, God's ways are often
beyond our understanding. On 4:2, Calvin writes: "Let us hence learn not
to arrogate to ourselves judgment in matters which exceed our capacities,
but to subject our minds to God, and to seek of him the spirit of wisdom."[50]
And on Jonah's expressed death wish in 4:3: "This example ought to check
us, that we express not too boldly our opinion respecting the doings of
God, but, on the contrary, hold our thoughts captive, lest any presump-
tion of this kind be manifested by us."[51]

The dominant theme that comes through Calvin's exposition is that of
the love and mercy of God. This is well illustrated in the final prayer of
the Jonah series:

> Grant, Almighty God, that as thou hast, in various ways, testified, and
> daily continuest to testify, how dear and precious to thee are mankind,
> and as we enjoy daily so many and so remarkable proofs of thy goodness
> and favour, — O grant, that we may learn to rely wholly on thy goodness,
> many examples of which thou settest before us, and which thou wouldest
> have us continually to experience, that we may not only pass through
> our earthly course, but also confidently aspire to the hope of that blessed
> and celestial life which is laid up for us in heaven, through Christ our
> Lord. Amen.[52]

Calvin's exposition always includes application to the lives of the hearers.
These applications appear throughout the text. A few examples: When
Jonah disobeyed God's call to go to Nineveh, Calvin says:

> It is a genuine proof of obedience when we simply obey God, however
> numerous the obstacles which may meet us and may be suggested to
> our minds, and though no escape may appear to us; yea, when we follow

---

[48] Calvin, *Minor Prophets,* 58.

[49] Calvin, *Minor Prophets,* 137–138.

[50] Calvin, *Minor Prophets,* 120–121.

[51] Calvin, *Minor Prophets,* 128.

[52] Calvin, *Minor Prophets,* 145.

God, as it were with closed eyes, wherever he may lead us, and doubt not but that he will add strength to us, and stretch forth also his hand, whenever need may require, to remove all our difficulties.[53]

Or, commenting on the Lord's care for the slumbering Jonah:

We hence see that the Lord often cares for his people when they care not for themselves, and that he watches while they are asleep.[54]

Jonah can become an example of piety. Calvin comments on 1:10: "But as Jonah here calmly answers, and raises no clamor, and shows no bitterness, so let every one of us, in the true spirit of meekness, acknowledge our own sins."[55]

Finally, Calvin's exposition relates the themes of the book to the classic teachings of the church. Commenting on Jonah's wish to see the temple once again, expressed from within the great fish, Calvin speaks of Baptism and the Lord's Supper:

We hence see that he thus encouraged himself to entertain good hope in his extreme necessity. And this is a useful admonition; for when every access to God seems closed up against us, nothing is more useful than to recall to mind, that he has adopted us from our very infancy, that he has also testified his favour by many tokens, especially that he has called us by his Gospel into a fellowship with his only-begotten Son, who is life and salvation; and then, that he has confirmed his favour both by Baptism and the Supper.[56]

In sum, here is a theocentric exposition of Jonah, reflecting something of the liveliness of encounter with a real audience, and applying the prophetic message to the hearers in a practical way.

---

[53] Calvin, *Minor Prophets*, 24.
[54] Calvin, *Minor Prophets*, 39.
[55] Calvin, *Minor Prophets*, 54.
[56] Calvin, *Minor Prophets*, 80–81.